SONGS OF WORK AND PROTEST

By

EDITH FOWKE

and

JOE GLAZER

Music Arrangements: **KENNETH BRAY**

Dover Publications, Inc., New York

Copyright

Copyright © 1973 by Dover Publications, Inc.
Copyright © 1960 by Labor Education Division of Roosevelt University.
All rights reserved.

Bibliographical Note

This Dover edition, first published in 1973, is an unabridged and corrected republication of the work originally published in 1960 by the Labor Education Division of Roosevelt University under the title *Songs of Work and Freedom*.

International Standard Book Number

ISBN-13: 978-0-486-22899-0
ISBN-10: 0-486-22899-1

Library of Congress Catalog Card Number: 72-86065

Manufactured in the United States by RR Donnelley
228899103   2015
www.doverpublications.com

PREFACE

It is with a sense of genuine achievement that the Labor Education Division of Roosevelt University has made possible the publication of this wonderful book, "Songs of Work and Protest," by Joe Glazer, Education Director of the United Rubber Workers, AFL-CIO, and the Canadian folklorist, Edith Fowke.

It is five years since Joe Glazer first presented the proposal to a meeting of our National Labor Advisory Committee that the Division publish such a book.

The Committee approved the idea unanimously. It took five years of research and organization to launch the book.

During all that time we have been in close consultation with the authors, suggesting additions, deletions, omissions—so that the final product would be what all of us have wanted for many years: a song book from the pages of which would emerge in true perspective the stirring sounds and deep emotions of peoples over hundreds of years on the march to build a better world. We think the authors have achieved this without sacrificing one jot of authenticity or painstaking scholarly research.

This is no book for resting on a quiet library shelf. It will be in constant use—well-thumbed —as union men and women and their children sing to piano or guitar at home, at union meetings, at summer schools in this country, and, we predict, in other countries of the world.

It will make available for the first time to scholars of folklore and social movements a wealth of fascinating material, until this time scattered, sparse, and unrelated—known only to a few of us who over the years have sung and preserved the words, music, and stories of work and freedom songs as we heard them sung in times of industrial crisis, political turmoil, or just plain singing joy.

The Labor Education Division of Roosevelt University extends its warm thanks to the several thousands of union members, to the local unions, to the international unions, to friends of the labor movement in universities and elsewhere, and to the devoted "fans" of Joe Glazer and Edith Fowke who responded to our appeal for advance orders so that the publication might be financed. Without you, we could not have done it.

Our special appreciation to the Labor Education Division office staff, Joyce Barnett, Robina Furness, Gloria Mims and Saki Miyashiro who handled the orders, manned the mimeograph, proofread manuscript, humming the songs as they worked.

We know you will agree with us that this book, "Songs of Work and Protest," was worth waiting for, so let's turn the pages now and sing out loud and clear.

FRANK MCCALLISTER, *Director*
AGNES M. DOUTY, *Assistant Director*
Labor Education Division
Roosevelt University
Chicago, Illinois

DEDICATION

To the men and women throughout the world who work in mine and mill, in field and factory, on sea and on the railroads, we dedicate this rich heritage of song and story about themselves, their despairs, their aspirations.

TABLE OF CONTENTS

Introduction 9

I. SOLIDARITY FOREVER

1. Solidarity Forever 12
2. The Commonwealth of Toil..................................... 14
3. Union Maid 17
4. Joe Hill 20
5. Talking Union 22
6. You've Got to Go Down and Join the Union.................... 25
7. The Eight Hour Day 26
8. Get Thee Behind Me, Satan................................... 28
9. Brother John 29

II. ON THE LINE

10. On the Line... 30
11. Hinky Dinky Parlez-vous...................................... 31
12. We Will Overcome... 33
13. Union Train 34
14. Hold the Fort... 36
15. We Shall Not Be Moved....................................... 38
16. Great Day 40
17. Old Ma Bell 42
18. Casey Jones 43
19. Roll the Union On.. 44
20. The Scabs Crawl In... 46

III. DOWN IN A COAL MINE

21. Down in a Coal Mine.. 47
22. Dark as a Dungeon.. 49
23. Sixteen Tons 52
24. Which Side Are You On?....................................... 54
25. The West Virginia Hills....................................... 56
26. The Death of Mother Jones.................................... 58
27. The Blantyre Explosion 60
28. Union Man 62
29. My Sweetheart's the Mule in the Mines........................ 64
30. A Miner's Life 65

IV. HARD TIMES IN THE MILL

31. Hard Times in the Mill.. 68
32. Bread and Roses.. 70
33. We Are Building a Strong Union............................... 72
34. The Winnsboro Cotton Mill Blues.............................. 74
35. The Mill Was Made of Marble................................. 76
36. The Anthem of the ILGWU.................................... 78

V. TAKE THIS HAMMER

37. Take This Hammer... 80
38. John Henry 82
39. Pat Works on the Railway...................................... 84
40. Drill Ye Tarriers, Drill....................................... 86
41. Jerry, Go and Oil that Car.................................... 88
42. The UAW-CIO 90
43. United Steelworkers Are We................................... 92

VI. MEN OF THE SOIL

44. Men of the Soil... 94
45. The Farmer Is the Man.. 96
46. The Boll Weevil... 98
47. Down on Penny's Farm.. 100
48. Planting Rice 102
49. Eleven Cent Cotton... 104

50. Zum Gali Gali.. 106
51. So Long, It's Been Good to Know You........................... 107
52. One Happy Swede... 110

VII. BLOW YE WINDS IN THE MORNING

53. Blow Ye Winds in the Morning................................... 112
54. Leave Her, Johnny... 114
55. Low Bridge, Everybody Down..................................... 115
56. Canaday-I-O... 118
57. The Buffalo Skinners.. 120
58. The Old Chisholm Trail... 122

VIII. HARD TRAVELING

59. Hard Traveling 124
60. Hallelujah, I'm a Bum.. 126
61. Going Down the Road Feeling Bad............................... 128
62. The Soup Song.. 130
63. Beans, Bacon, and Gravy... 132
64. Fourpence a Day.. 134
65. Life Is a Toil... 136
66. Acres of Clams... 138
67. The Teacher's Lament... 141
68. Too Old to Work.. 143
69. Automation 146

IX. THE RICH MAN AND THE POOR MAN

70. The Rich Man and the Poor Man................................. 148
71. The Dodger 150
72. No Irish Need Apply.. 152
73. Times Is Mighty Hard.. 154
74. The Preacher and the Slave....................................... 155
75. The Man that Waters the Workers' Beer.......................... 158
76. I Don't Want Your Millions, Mister.............................. 160
77. The Song of the Guaranteed Wage............................... 162

X. O FREEDOM!

78. O Freedom! 164
79. We Are Marching On to Victory.................................. 165
80. The Abolitionist Hymn.. 167
81. Go Down, Moses.. 168
82. John Brown's Body.. 170
83. The Battle Hymn of the Republic................................ 172
84. No More Auction Block... 173

XI. THESE THINGS SHALL BE!

85. These Things Shall Be!... 174
86. The Cutty Wren... 175
87. Die Gedanken Sind Frei... 178
88. When Wilt Thou Save the People?................................ 180
89. A New Jerusalem.. 182
90. The Marseillaise 183
91. A Man's a Man for a' That....................................... 186
92. Jefferson and Liberty... 188
93. The Red Flag... 190
94. The Peatbog Soldiers... 192
95. Kevin Barry.. 194
96. Let Us All Speak Our Minds..................................... 195
97. It Could Be a Wonderful World.................................. 198
98. Everybody Loves Saturday Night................................. 200
99. Hey Ho, Nobody Home... 201
100. Going to Study War No More.................................... 202

Record List 204

Reading List 206

Index 207

INTRODUCTION

"Sing and fight!" said the colorful Industrial Workers of the World, better known as the Wobblies. They told their members: "Right was the tyrant king who once said, 'Beware of a movement that sings.' . . . Whenever and wherever the oppressed challenge the old order, songs are on their lips."

It is not surprising, then, that songs of protest have a long history. We know that the French rebels marched on Paris to the strains of the Marseillaise, but what songs did the Children of Israel sing when Moses led them out of the land of bondage? What songs did the Thracian slaves sing when they challenged the might of Imperial Rome? How many great songs of revolt have been lost forever?

The oldest song in this book is "The Cutty Wren," dating from the Peasants' Revolt of 1381 against feudal oppression, nearly six hundred years ago. A recent one is "The Song of the Guaranteed Wage," less than six years old. In fourteenth-century England the peasants sang of killing the wren (i.e., the feudal lord) and distributing his wealth among the poor. In twentieth-century America the workers sing of improving their job security by negotiating a union contract with a guaranteed annual wage.

Six hundred years ago:

> "And who will get the spare-ribs?"
> "We'll give them all to the poor."

Six years ago:

> "And children at last you can live unafraid
> When you know that your daddy will always get paid."

The tactics and situations change, but the goal remains the same: a better life for ordinary people.

This book brings you the songs of the people who have fought for their rights on picket lines and battle fields, in prison and at the polls. Here are the songs of the men and women who raised their voices against political and industrial tyranny, against child labor, hunger, poverty, unemployment. Here are the songs of the oppressed, the downtrodden, the disinherited.

Here is the song of the textile millhand, working from "can't see to can't see," and of the coal miner who lusts "for the lure of the mine"; the song of the sailor in the strenuous days of the clipper ship who is "working mighty hard for mighty little pay," and of the itinerant worker of modern times who is "cutting that wheat, stacking that hay, trying to make 'bout a dollar a day."

Here are the Negroes fleeing from slavery who chant "No more auction block for me," and the prisoners in German concentration camps who dream of the day when they will "cry rejoicing, 'Homeland dear, you're mine at last!'" Here are the songs of an Irish rebel hanged by English soldiers, and of an American Wobbly shot in Utah; songs of men who struggled to "build a new Jerusalem in England's green and pleasant land," and of workers in the Philippine rice fields who "cannot stand, cannot sit, cannot rest a little bit."

The fight for freedom and a better life knows no boundaries and respects no barriers. It has its martyrs and its heroes, its leaders and its rank-and-file, and these are the songs that speak for them.

While some of the songs were created by poets of world renown, most of them sprang from the hearts of unlettered farmers and factory hands, of wandering Wobblies and ragged-trousered philosophers. The words are often rough and awkward, but what they lack in polish they make up in sincerity. Verses that sound clumsy and uninspired when read in the drawing-room were often extraordinarily effective when sung in the meeting hall or on the picket line.

Musicians may complain that many of the tunes are unimpressive, but most of them fulfill the prime requirement of a people's song: that it shall be easy to sing. A great many of the union song-writers borrowed their tunes from familiar folk songs, popular songs, or gospel hymns which were already known to the men for whom they were writing.

This book has two aims: to provide a good collection of songs that can be sung by trade unions and other interested groups, and to show how these songs reflect mankind's struggle for a better life. Many of them may seem old-fashioned to the modern reader, but they mark the milestones on the workers' long road toward freedom and justice. This singing history is a testament to man's enduring will to make this world a better place to live in.

We have tried as far as possible to choose those songs which have sprung directly from a genuine situation and which have at one time or another been fairly widely sung by ordinary people. Most of them come from the United States or Britain: we are sorry that we have had to leave out many fine protest songs from other countries because good singable English translations were not available.

Although many of our "Songs of Work and Protest" cannot be classed as folk songs, most of them have circulated largely by oral tradition and therefore exist in a number of more or less different versions. Even such recently composed numbers as Merle Travis's fine mining songs, "Sixteen Tons" and "Dark as a Dungeon," have undergone minor changes through this oral process. For that reason, readers may find that the versions given here differ somewhat from the ones they know. As far as possible, we have tried to choose the forms that express the spirit of the song and are best suited to group singing.

The notes that accompany each song tell how it orginated and sketch in the conditions that inspired it, thus helping to set the songs in their proper historical perspective. The origins of some songs are obscure, but every effort has been made to track down their sources.

The songs have been grouped into sections roughly corresponding to their subject, although there is inevitably some overlapping. The book opens with straight trade-union songs and ditties sung on the picket line, and goes on to the specific songs of the miners, the textile-workers, the steel and railway workers, and the farmers. Then comes a general section, "Blow Ye Winds of Morning," which gives typical work songs of such groups as the sailors, the canalers, the lumberjacks, and the cowboys. "Hard Travelling" emphasizes the hardships that working men—and women—have to face, particularly during times of depression, and "The Rich Man and the Poor Man" makes some philosophic and some ironic comments on the economic system. "O Freedom" contains some songs that grew out of the fight against slavery, and "These Things Shall Be!" is a broad section expressing the dreams of people of many lands throughout the ages.

Although many different types of songs are represented, the largest group—over a third of the entire collection—sprang from the American trade-union movement. American union songs fall roughly into three periods: the early songs (before 1900), the Wobbly songs (from the early 1900's to 1920), and the modern songs. Only a handful of complete songs and a few fragments have survived from the nineteenth century. They are represented here by "The Eight Hour Day" and "Hold the Fort."

The Wobblies, a great singing labor movement, were active from 1905 to the early 1920's. Wobblies wrote, published, and sang more than two hundred union songs, but only a few of these are still sung today. Most of them are outmoded because their appeal was strongly localized or because their fierce class-struggle content does not fit the modern labor movement. The best known Wobbly song is, of course, "Solidarity Forever." Other typical Wobbly songs included are "The Commonwealth of Toil," "Casey Jones," and "The Preacher and the Slave."

Most of the union songs in this book fall into what we have termed the modern period. This includes the years of the Great Depression and the explosive rise of industrial unionism in the 1930's.

The best union songs come out of the bitter times: the great struggles and the hard-fought strikes, out of triumphs won against overwhelming odds. Peaceful, prosperous times on the labor front rarely bring forth a song worth singing or saving. As John Steinbeck shrewdly remarked, "The greatest and most enduring songs are wrung from unhappy people—the spirituals of the slaves which say in effect, 'It is hopeless here, maybe in heaven it will be better'." In the great industrial struggles, the coal-miner says it is hopeless in the mine, the textile-worker says it is hopeless in the mill—but the union will make it better.

If one wonders why such a high proportion of good union songs come from the coal mines and textile mills, the answer is not hard to find. The textile-workers and the coal-miners have worked mostly in lonely mine-patches and mill villages, many of them located in the rural south or in isolated mountain communities. Many of these workers come from a great singing tradition—secular or religious, or both. Miners and mill-workers have had a long, fierce, and often tragic struggle to build a union. This combination of isolation, singing tradition, and bitter struggle has provided what might be called the perfect climate for the production of protest songs.

Does this mean that we can no longer expect any good songs to come out of the modern labor movement? Not necessarily. It will be more difficult to develop good rousing union songs in a movement that has become strong, well organized, and in many places respectable, and from a work force that has become more and more urbanized and less and less isolated. But the millenium has not yet arrived. Although we have come a long way, we still have with us the low-paid, the unorganized, and the exploited. We still face the spectre of unemployment and the threat of war. As long as men continue to struggle for a better world, they will need songs to encourage them in that struggle.

We are grateful to many people who have done pioneer work in the field of the protest song: to men like George Korson in the United States and A. L. Lloyd in England who collected the songs of the miners, to men like John and Alan Lomax and Carl Sandburg who collected many fine work songs, and to John Greenway who produced the first comprehensive history of *American Folk Songs of Protest.*

We wish to thank all the people who have given us information and helped us in many ways. Among these are Agnes Douty, Chester Graham, Archie Green, Lee Hays, Margaret Knight, Frank McCallister, Shirley McGuffey, John Neuhaus, Helen and Mark Starr, Peter Seeger, Irwin Silber, and Norris Tibbetts, and, most of all, our thanks to our spouses, Frank Fowke and Mildred Glazer, who showed monumental patience and forbearance during the five years this book was in the making.

EDITH FOWKE and JOE GLAZER

SOLIDARITY FOREVER

Words by RALPH CHAPLIN

1. When the union's inspiration through the workers' blood shall run,
   There can be no power greater anywhere beneath the sun.
   Yet what force on earth is weaker than the feeble strength of one?
   But the union makes us strong.

   CHORUS: Solidarity forever!
   Solidarity forever!
   Solidarity forever!
   For the union makes us strong.

2. They have taken untold millions that they never toiled to earn,
   But without our brain and muscle not a single wheel could turn.
   We can break their haughty power, gain our freedom when we learn
   That the union makes us strong

3. In our hands is placed a power greater than their hoarded gold,
   Greater than the might of armies magnified a thousand fold.
   We can bring to birth a new world from the ashes of the old,
   For the union makes us strong.

"Solidarity Forever" is the most popular union song on the North American continent. If a union member knows only one union song it is almost sure to be this. It has become, in effect, the anthem of the American labor movement.

Ralph Chaplin, the famous poet, artist, writer, and organizer for the Industrial Workers of the World, wrote "Solidarity Forever" on January 17, 1915. That day, while lying on the rug in his living room, he scribbled stanza after stanza. The idea had come to him earlier while he was in West Virginia helping the coal miners in the great Kanawha Valley strike. Little did he dream then that song would live on after all his other work was forgotten.

Chaplin recalls: "I wanted a song to be full of revolutionary fervor and to have a chorus that was singing and defiant." He achieved exactly this effect by combining his militant lyrics with the stirring Civil War tune of "John Brown's Body."

Chaplin actually wrote six verses, but the three given here are the ones usually sung today. The other verses are of historical interest but sound rather out-of-date to present-day union members.

THE COMMONWEALTH OF TOIL

Words by RALPH CHAPLIN

Hopefully

In the gloom of migh - ty ci - ties, midst the roar of whir - ling wheels, we are

toil - ing on like chat - tel slaves of old, _____ And our mas - ters hope to

keep us e - ver thus be - neath their heels, and to coin our ve - ry life-blood in - to

gold. _____ But we have a glow - ing dream of how fair the world will

1. In the gloom of mighty cities,
   Mid the roar of whirling wheels,
   We are toiling on like chattel slaves of old,
   And our masters hope to keep us
   Ever thus beneath their heels,
   And to coin our very life blood into gold.

CHORUS: But we have a glowing dream
   Of how fair the world will seem
   When each man can live his life secure and free;
   When the earth is owned by labor
   And there's joy and peace for all
   In the Commonwealth of Toil that is to be.

(over)

2. They would keep us cowed and beaten,
   Cringing meekly at their feet.
   They would stand between each worker and his bread.
   Shall we yield our lives up to them
   For the bitter crust we eat?
   Shall we only hope for heaven when we're dead?

3. They have laid our lives out for us
   To the utter end of time.
   Shall we stagger on beneath their heavy load?
   Shall we let them live forever
   In their gilded halls of crime,
   With our children doomed to toil beneath their goad?

4. When our cause is all triumphant
   And we claim our Mother Earth,
   And the nightmare of the present fades away,
   We shall live with love and laughter,
   We who now are little worth,
   And we'll not regret the price we have to pay.

In 1905 the Industrial Workers of the World (IWW) was organized in Chicago. The IWW—soon nicknamed the "Wobblies"—set out to organize the "downtrodden" and the "dispossessed," that large body of unskilled workers of factory and field who were generally considered unorganizable by the American Federation of Labor, then the major trade-union organization in the United States.

The Wobblies knew how to use the power of music and poetry to agitate and organize. In 1908 or 1909 (the exact date is not certain), they published the first edition of their "Little Red Song Book" which went on to sell thousands of copies each year. On its cover it carried the slogan: "IWW Songs—To Fan the Flames of Discontent." In 1956, the twenty-ninth edition appeared to commemorate the fiftieth anniversary of the IWW—although the IWW as an organization is now only a handful of old men living on the memory of their turbulent past.

During most of the years that the IWW was active it was hardly necessary to "fan the flames of discontent" with militant songs and stirring music; wretched economic conditions did the fanning. The heavy hand of government was inevitably on the side of the employer and the right to organize and build unions had to be fought out on bloodied picket lines.

Skilled tradesmen found their place in the unions of the American Federation of Labor. But large masses of workers, laboring in forsaken centers of industry, had no voice. These included immigrant textile workers in the East, rough and tough lumberjacks in the Northwest, migratory workers who followed the crops, and miners on the Mesabi Range in Minnesota.

To these exploited groups the IWW offered hope of a better and brighter tomorrow. "Sing and fight!" was their cry, and many Wobbly poets shaped their grievances into songs. Some of the best known were T-Bone Slim, Harry McClintock, Richard Brazier, Joe Hill, and Ralph Chaplin.

Ralph Chaplin wrote, and thousands of Wobblies sang of the day "when the earth is owned by labor and there's joy and peace for all in the commonwealth of toil that is to be." Like Chaplin's more famous song, "Solidarity Forever," "The Commonwealth of Toil" was set to a familiar tune—this time, "Darling Nelly Gray." Although it is rarely heard today, it remains a good example of the many stirring songs produced by the Wobblies.

UNION MAID

Words by WOODY GUTHRIE
and the ALMANAC SINGERS

With spirit

There once was a u-nion maid; She ne-ver was a-fraid Of

goons and ginks and com-pa-ny finks And the de-pu-ty she-riffs that made the raid. She

went to the u-nion hall when a meet-ing it was called, And when the com-p'ny

boys came 'round she al-ways stood her ground. Oh, you can't scare

1. There once was a union maid;
   She never was afraid
   Of goons and ginks and company finks
   And the deputy sheriffs that made the raid.
   She went to the union hall
   When a meeting it was called,
   And when the company boys came 'round
   She always stood her ground.

CHORUS: Oh, you can't scare me, I'm sticking to the union.
   I'm sticking to the union, I'm sticking to the union.
   Oh, you can't scare me, I'm sticking to the union,
   I'm sticking to the union till the day I die.

2. This union maid was wise
   To the tricks of company spies;
   She couldn't be fooled by company stools;
   She'd always organize the guys.
   She'd always get her way
   When she struck for higher pay;
   She'd show her card to the National Guard
   And this is what she'd say:

3. You girls who want to be free
   Just take a tip from me!
   Get you a man who's a union man
   And join the Ladies' Auxiliary.
   Married life ain't hard
   When you've got a union card.
   A union man has a happy life
   When he's got a union wife.

There is sometimes a tendency to ignore the role that women—both as workers and as wives of union men—have played in helping to build the labor movement.

As early as 1834, women textile workers in Lowell, Massachusetts struck against wage cuts. They proclaimed: "As our fathers resisted unto blood the lordly avarice of the British Ministry, so we, their daughters, never will wear the yoke which has been prepared for us." These girls marched through the streets of Lowell singing:

"Oh, isn't it a pity that such a pretty girl as I
Should be sent to the factory to pine away and die?
Oh, I cannot be a slave,
For I'm so fond of liberty."

Seventy-five years later, 20,000 shirtwaist-makers—mostly women—struck for three months against intolerable conditions in New York City sweatshops. Most of these girls were Jewish immigrants. They raised their right arms and took the old Jewish oath: "If I turn traitor to the cause I now pledge, may this hand wither from the arm I now raise."

Mother Jones, Fanny Sellins, Sara Ogan, Aunt Molly Jackson, and others did noble work in the great miners' struggles.

Joe Hill glorified the "Rebel Girl" whose "hands may be hardened by labor" in typical, colorful Wobbly style:

"That's the Rebel Girl, that's the Rebel Girl,
To the working class she's a precious pearl.
She brings courage, pride, and joy
To the fighting rebel boy."

In more modern times, the telephone workers' union (Communications Workers of America), made up 80 per cent of women, has established a dynamic, democratic union and has taken on the giant telephone company in many hard-fought strikes.

But the woman who is the unsung hero of the labor movement is the "union widow"—the wife of the devoted trade unionist who spends many an evening and long weekend without her man. She keeps a home and raises a family while her union man is organizing, negotiating, attending meetings: local union or district meetings, council meetings, conferences, conventions.

Sam Gompers, first president of the AFL, wrote about his early work in the 1880's: "More often than not it was midnight before I got home—there were meetings, speeches to make, conferences to attend, for the cause of labor is no easy mistress to serve . . ."

Woody Guthrie's "Union Maid" is the best known song about women in the labor movement. Peter Seeger reports: "We were in Oklahoma City in 1940 at a union meeting. Many of the men had brought their wives. The company had sent around some toughs to intimidate the workers. But the workers held their ground. The next morning Woody had typed out 'Union Maid' to the tune of 'Red Wing.' Millard Lampell (one of the Almanac Singers) supplied the third verse."

"Union Maid" quickly became—and remained—one of the half-dozen most popular union songs.

JOE HILL

Music by EARL ROBINSON
Words by ALFRED HAYES

Somewhat slow, with feeling

1. I dreamed I saw Joe Hill last night
   Alive as you and me.
   Says I, "But Joe, you're ten years dead."
   "I never died," says he.
   "I never died," says he.

2. "In Salt Lake, Joe, by God," says I,
   Him standing by my bed,
   "They framed you on a murder charge."
   Says Joe, "But I ain't dead."
   Says Joe, "But I ain't dead."

3. "The copper bosses killed you, Joe,
   They shot you, Joe," says I.
   "Takes more than guns to kill a man,"
   Says Joe, "I didn't die."
   Says Joe, "I didn't die."

4. And standing there as big as life
   And smiling with his eyes,
   Joe says, "What they forgot to kill
   Went on to organize.
   Went on to organize."

5. "Joe Hill ain't dead," he says to me,
   "Joe Hill ain't never died.
   Where working men are out on strike
   Joe Hill is at their side.
   Joe Hill is at their side."

6. "From San Diego up to Maine
   In every mine and mill,
   Where workers strike and organize,"
   Says he, "You'll find Joe Hill."
   Says he, "You'll find Joe Hill."

7. I dreamed I saw Joe Hill last night
   Alive as you and me.
   Says I, "But Joe, you're ten years dead."
   "I never died," says he.
   "I never died," says he.

"It was Joe Hill more than any other song-writer who made the Industrial Workers of the World a singing organization." That was the verdict of Ralph Chaplin, author of "Solidarity Forever" and a leading IWW poet and song-writer himself.

Who was this Joe Hill about whose death—and life—so many books, articles, songs, and poems have been written?

Joe Hill—born Joel Emmanuel Hagglund in Sweden—came to the United States in 1901 when he was nineteen. In 1910, he became an active member of the Wobblies on the West Coast when he was working in the port of San Pedro.

Joe had a poetic streak in him and liked to pick out tunes on the piano. His name became known among Wobblies and other trade unionists when he wrote "Casey Jones," "The Preacher and the Slave," and many other popular union songs. He sang his songs at union meetings, on street corners, and on picket lines, and they became so popular that the 1913 edition of the IWW's famous "Little Red Song Book" contained no less than thirteen of them.

In January, 1914, Hill was arrested in Salt Lake City, Utah, on a murder charge. Despite the intervention of President Woodrow Wilson and the Swedish government, despite the condemnation of the trial as unfair by the American Federation of Labor, despite vigorous protests from public meetings throughout the country and as far away as Australia, Joe Hill was finally executed by a five-man firing squad on November 19, 1915.

The case of Joe Hill is still being debated. In their books, *The Preacher and the Slave* and *American Folk Songs of Protest*, Wallace Stegner and John Greenway present arguments to tear down the "myth" of Joe Hill as a great labor hero and martyr, implying that Hill was the kind of fellow who might have committed the murder with which he was charged. Further evidence for this point of view is presented by Professor Vernon Jensen of Cornell University in an article, "The Legend of Joe Hill," which appeared in the *Industrial & Labor Relations Review* in April, 1951. However, this theory is vigorously disputed by Barrie Stavis who presents a mass of documented evidence in his book, *The Man Who Never Died,* to show that Hill was innocent and that he was the victim of a frame-up because he was a militant trade unionist and a well-known Wobbly.

The day before Joe Hill was executed in Salt Lake City, he sent a wire to Wobbly leader Big Bill Haywood at IWW headquarters in Chicago. Hill's words were to become famous: "Don't waste time mourning. Organize."

Hill's body was brought to Chicago where 30,000 sympathizers marched in one of the greatest funeral processions ever seen in that or any other city. Eulogies were delivered in nine languages. Then, in keeping with Joe's wishes, his body was cremated. His ashes were placed in many small envelopes and scattered throughout the United States and in countries on every continent. But no ashes were dropped in the State of Utah because Joe "did not want to be found dead there."

The night before Joe Hill was shot, a speaker at a protest meeting in Salt Lake City cried: "Joe Hill will never die!" And in a way he never did die because he has become a symbol of the hundreds of men and women who have been killed while battling for labor's rights.

Perhaps the most important factor in perpetuating his memory is this moving song which was written by Earl Robinson and Alfred Hayes some twenty years after his death.

TALKING UNION

Talking blues, steady beat.

Words by the ALMANAC SINGERS

If you want high-er wa-ges, let me tell you what to do, you've got to talk to the wor-kers in the shop with you. You've got to build you a u-nion, got to make it strong, But if you all stick to-ge-ther, boys, 'twon't be long, You'll get shor-ter hours, bet-ter wor-king con-di-tions, Va-

ca-tions with pay, take your kids to the sea-shore It ain't

If you want higher wages, let me tell you what to do,
You've got to talk to the workers in the shop with you.
You've got to build you a union, got to make it strong,
But if you all stick together, boys, 'twon't be long —
You'll get shorter hours . . . better working conditions . . .
Vacations with pay . . . take your kids to the seashore.

    It ain't quite this simple, so I'd better explain
    Just why you've got to ride on the union train,
    'Cause if you wait for the boss to raise your pay
    We'll all be a-waiting till the judgment day —
    We'll all be buried . . . gone to heaven . . .
    St. Peter'll be the foreman then.

Now you know you're underpaid but the boss says you ain't,
He speeds up the work till you're about to faint.
You may be down and out, but you ain't beaten —
You can pass out a leaflet and call a meetin' —
Talk it over . . . speak your mind . . .
Decide to do something about it.

    'Course, the boss may persuade some poor damn fool
    To go to your meeting and act like a stool,
    But you can always tell a stool, boys, that's a fact,
    He's got a yellow streak a-running down his back.
    He doesn't have to stool . . . he'll always get along . . .
    On what he steals out of blind men's cups.

You've got a union now and you're sitting pretty;
Put some of the boys on the bargaining committee.
The boss won't listen when one guy squawks
But he's got to listen when the union talks.
He'd better . . . be mighty lonely . . .
If everybody decided to walk out on him.

    Suppose they're working you so hard it's just outrageous,
    And they're paying you all starvation wages.
    You go to the boss, and the boss will yell
    "Before I raise your pay I'll see you all in Hell."

(over)

He's puffing a big seegar, feeling mighty slick
'Cause he thinks he's got your union licked.
Well, he looks out the window, and what does he see
But a thousand pickets, and they all agree
He's a bastard . . . unfair . . . slave-driver . . .
Bet he beats his wife.

> Now, boys, you've come to the hardest time.
> The boss will try to bust your picket line.
> He'll call out the po-lice and the National Guard;
> They'll tell you it's a crime to have a union card;
> They'll raid your meetings, they'll hit you on the head —
> They'll call every one of you a Goddamn Red —
> Unpatriotic . . agitators . . .
> Send 'em back where they came from.

But out in De-troit, here's what they found,
And out in Pittsburgh, here's what they found,
And out in Akron, here's what they found,
And up in Toronto, here's what they found:
That if you don't let Red-baiting break you up,
And if you don't let vigilantes break you up,
And if you don't let race hatred break you up,
And if you don't let stool-pigeons break you up,
You'll win . . . what I mean . . .
Take it easy . . . but take it!

"Talking Union" is one of the best organizing speeches ever made. Written not to be sung but to be spoken in the traditional style of the talking blues, this "speech" must be delivered with musical accompaniment and a steady, swinging beat.

"Talking Union" is patterned on a Negro spiritual which began: "If you want to get to heaven let me tell you what to do." It was written in the early 1940's mainly by Peter Seeger and Millard Lampell, with some assistance from Lee Hays. At that time they were all members of the Almanac Singers, a group of young folk singers who wrote or popularized many fine union songs, including "Union Maid," "Which Side Are You On?", "Union Train," "Get Thee Behind Me, Satan," and "I Don't Want Your Millions, Mister." The personnel of the Almanac Singers varied from time to time, but its best known members were Seeger, Guthrie, Hays, and Lampell.

YOU'VE GOT TO GO DOWN

Words and music by
WOODY GUTHRIE

With steady beat

(over)

1. You've got to go down and join the union —
   You've got to join it for yourself.
   There ain't nobody going to join it for you —
   You've got to to go down and join the union for yourself.

2. Sister's got to go down and join the union —
   She's got to join it for herself.
   There ain't nobody going to join it for her —
   She's got to go down and join the union for herself.

3. Brother's got to go down and join the union —
   He's got to join it for himself.
   There ain't nobody going to join it for him —
   He's got to go down and join the union for himself.

4. Everybody's going down to join the union —
   They've got to join it for themselves.
   There ain't nobody going to join it for them —
   They've got to go down and join the union for themselves.

This simple but effective union parody of the spiritual, "I've Got To Walk My Lonesome Valley," was written by Woody Guthrie in 1946.

THE EIGHT HOUR DAY

work both late and ear - ly, and get but lit - tle pay play;
To sup-
hours we'd have for work - ing, Eight hours we'd have for
Eight

port our wives and chil - dren in free A - mer - i - kay.
hours we'd have for sleep - ing in free A - mer - i - kay.

In 1853, the time table of the Holyoke Mills in Massachusetts called for the following work schedule: "Ring in at 5 A.M. Ring out at 6:30 P.M." One-half hour was allowed for breakfast and one-half hour for lunch.

We have come a long way since those twelve- and fourteen-hour work days of a hundred years ago. Every decade several hours have been chipped off the average week. The record of progress is slow, but certain:

1850...average work week 70 hours
1900...average work week 60 hours
1920...average work week 50 hours
1955...average work week 40 hours

But the march of progress has not been easy. Employers fought bitterly against the reduction of hours from 12 to 10 and from 10 to 8, just as they are currently fighting labor's efforts to cut hours below the standard 40-hour week. In the 1840's when unions were attempting to win the ten-hour day, one employer declared:

> "The morals of the operatives will necessarily suffer if longer absent from the wholesome discipline of factory life, and leaving them thus to their will and liberty, without a warrant that this time will be well employed."

After the Civil War workers began to agitate for the eight-hour day. Ira Steward was the moving spirit of the eight-hour movement. He maintained that hours could be reduced without cutting wages, and he used this jingle to publicize his point:

> "Whether you work by the piece or work by the day
> Decreasing the hours increases the pay."

Much of the eight-hour agitation culminated in strikes and demonstrations across the country on May 1, 1886. This was the first time May Day had been celebrated by organized workers.

This song, "The Eight Hour Day," set to the tune of "The British Grenadiers," originated among the miners and was probably used during their 1897 strike in which the eight-hour day was the issue. It was not until 1938, with the passage of the Wage and Hour Law, that the eight-hour day became firmly established in the United States.

GET THEE BEHIND ME, SATAN

Words and music by
ALMANAC SINGERS

Blues style

The boss comes up to me with a five dol-lar bill; says, "Get you some whis key, boy, and

CHORUS

drink your fill." Get thee be - hind me, Sa - tan, tra - vel on down the line.

I am a u - nion man, Gon-na leave you be - hind.

A -

1. The boss came up to me with a five-dollar bill,
   Says, "Get you some whiskey, boy, and drink your fill."
   CHORUS: Get thee behind me, Satan,
   Travel on down the line.
   I am a union man,
   Gonna leave you behind.

2. A red-headed woman took me out to dine,
   Says, "Love me, baby, leave your union behind."

3. On the Fourth of July the politicians say:
   "Vote for us, and we will raise your pay."

4. Oh, then the company union sent out a call,
   Said, "Join us in the summer, we'll forget you in the fall."

5. If anyone should ask you your union to sell,
   Just tell him where to go, send him back to Hell.

The company union, the company stooge, and the company spy have always been targets for the most vigorous attacks by loyal trade-unionists. This rousing blast at those who would sell out the union is another product of the Almanac Singers who first sang it for striking Ford workers in Detroit in 1941. Lee Hays wrote most of it, with a little help from Peter Seeger and Millard Lampell.

BROTHER JOHN

Are you sleep-ing, are you sleep-ing, Bro-ther John, Bro-ther John?

Up and join the u-nion, up and join the u-nion, A-F-L, C-I-O.

The popular French round, "Frère Jacques," is well known in many countries and is sung throughout the United States and Canada in both English and French. The version given here probably found its way into the American labor movement during the great organizing drives conducted by the CIO in the late 1930's. The initials in the last line are usually changed to fit the particular union that is singing it at the time.

ON THE LINE

The u-nion is the place for me, the place for work-ing men, Who

want some time to sing and play and mo-ney they can spend. On the

CHORUS

line (on the line), on the line (on the line), Come and pic-ket on the pic-ket

line. We'll win our fight, our fight for the right, on the pic-ket, pic-ket line.

1. The union is the place for me,
   The place for working men
   Who want some time to sing and play
   And money they can spend.

CHORUS:
   On the line (on the line),
   On the line (on the line),
   Come and picket on the picket line.
   We'll win our fight,
   Our fight for the right,
   On the picket, picket line.

2. I am a union man because
   I want a living wage;
   We'll stick together, we'll fight together,
   We'll get that living wage.

3. To win our strike and our demands
   Come and picket on the picket line.
   In one strong union we'll join hands
   On the picket, picket line.

This song was sung at least as far back as 1926 during the famous textile strike at Passaic, New Jersey.

Agnes Martocci Douty, who has sung union songs on many a picket line, first heard "On The Line" in 1927 or 1928 in New York City when she and some classmates from Hunter College turned out to help an early morning picket line for the International Ladies' Garment Workers' Union. It is one of the most popular of the many picket-line songs set to familiar tunes — in this case, "Polly Wolly Doodle."

HINKY DINKY PARLEZ VOUS

The bos-ses are tak-ing it on the chin, par - lez - vou's, ——— The

bos - ses are tak-ing it on the chin, par - lez - vous, ——— The

(over)

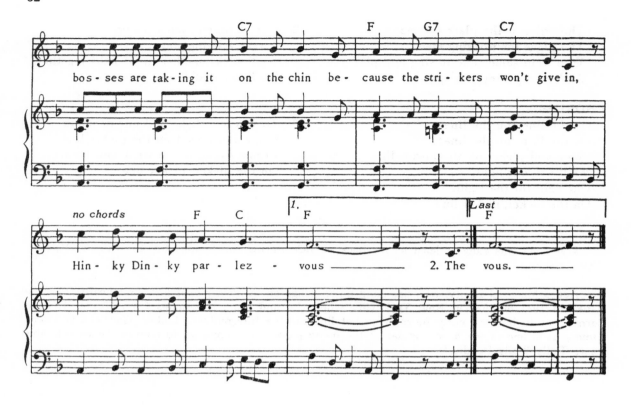

bos - ses are tak - ing it on the chin be - cause the stri - kers won't give in,

Hin - ky Din - ky par - lez - vous ———— 2. The vous. ————

1. The bosses are taking it on the chin, parley-vous,
   The bosses are taking it on the chin, parley-vous,
   The bosses are taking it on the chin because the strikers won't give in,
   Hinky dinky parley-vous.

2. The scabs are having a heck of a time, parley-vous,
   The scabs are having a heck of a time, parley-vous,
   The scabs are having a heck of a time trying to cross the picket line,
   Hinky dinky parley-vous.

3. The boss is shaking at the knees, parley-vous,
   The boss is shaking at the knees, parley-vous,
   The boss is shaking at the knees; he's shaking in his B.V.D.'s,
   Hinky dinky parley-vous.

4. We're going to win the union shop, parley-vous,
   We're going to win the union shop, parley-vous,
   We're going to win the union shop; we'll clean the floor with a union mop,
   Hinky dinky parley-vous.

5. We're staying on the picket line, parley-vous,
   We're staying on the picket line, parley-vous,
   We're staying on the picket line until we get the boss to sign,
   Hinky dinky parley-vous.

The rollicking rhythm of "Mademoiselle from Armentières" made it a favorite among the Allied soldiers in World War I. Following the war American workers borrowed the tune for this picket-line chant which is still used today.

WE WILL OVERCOME

1. We will overcome, we will overcome,
   We will overcome some day.
   Oh, down in my heart I do believe
   We will overcome some day.

2. We will organize, we will organize,
   We will organize some day.
   Oh, down in my heart I do believe
   We will organize some day.

3. We will build a new world, we will build a
      new world,
   We will build a new world some day.
   Oh, down in my heart I do believe
   We will build a new world some day.

4. We will overcome, we will overcome,
   We will overcome some day.
   Oh, down in my heart I do believe
   We will overcome some day.

(over)

Musically speaking, the line from the church to the union hall is very often short and direct. Some of the greatest union songs have been adapted from hymns, gospel songs, and spirituals.

This is especially true in the South where children are singing hymns as soon as they can talk. The combination of the great hymn-singing tradition in the Bible-belt South and the influence of the Negro spiritual on the one hand, and the hard-bitten employer opposition to unionism on the other, created the perfect climate for workers' self-expression through union songs during periods of industrial strife.

The workers quite naturally transferred their music and their feelings from the church to the union hall or picket line. In the West Virginia coal fields, "Jesus is my Captain, I shall not be moved," is readily changed to "Frank Keeney is my Captain, we shall not be moved." The spirit and the emotion is the same. The Lord will save us in church, but the union, the union leader Frank Keeney, will save us on the picket line.

In Marion, North Carolina, "We Are Climbing Jacob's Ladder" becomes "We Are Building A Strong Union." In Tennessee, "Great Day, the Righteous Marching" is changed to "Great Day, the Union's Marching." A group of colored and white textile workers in a union school in the Smoky Mountains, North Carolina, obviously affected by the bond of brotherhood built by their union, gather around the piano and sing: "Since I been introduced to the CIO, I ain't no stranger now" — a simple variation of the original, "Since I been introduced to the House of the Lord."

"We Will Overcome" is another fine song in this tradition. Zilphia Horton of the Highlander Folk School in Tennessee learned it in 1947 from the members of the Food and Tobacco Workers' Union who were attending the school. Mrs. Horton wrote: "It was first sung in Charleston, South Carolina, and one of the stanzas of the original hymn was 'We Will Overcome.' At school here they naturally added other verses. Its strong emotional appeal and simple dignity never fail to hit people."

UNION TRAIN

com - ing, What is that I _____ see yon - der com - ing, com - ing,

com - ing, Get on board, _____ Get on board. _____

1. Oh, what is that I see yonder coming, coming, coming,
Oh, what is that I see yonder coming, coming, coming,
What is that I see yonder coming, coming, coming?
Get on board! Get on board!

2. It's that union train a-coming, coming, coming,) 3
Get on board! Get on board!

3. It has saved a-many a thousand, thousand, thousand,) 3
Get on board! Get on board!

4. It will carry us to freedom, freedom, freedom,) 3
Get on board! Get on board!

5. What is that I see yonder coming, coming, coming,) 3
Get on board! Get on board!

6. It's that union train a-coming, coming, coming,) 3
Get on board! Get on board!

During the 1930's the Southern Tenant Farmers' Union began to organize the sharecroppers and farm laborers in the rich cotton country of the Mississippi delta. Many of these workers were Negroes, and at their union meetings they sang the hymns they had known from childhood. At one such meeting near Memphis, Tennessee, after they had sung the spiritual, "The Old Ship of Zion," a woman at the back started singing a new verse to the familiar tune. Later Lee Hays added more verses, and thus the "Union Train" began to roll.

HOLD THE FORT

Music by PHILIP P. BLISS

With determination

We meet to-day in free-dom's cause and raise our voi-ces high; We'll
join our hands in u-nion strong to bat-tle or to die.

CHORUS

Hold the fort for we are com-ing, U-nion men be strong,
Side by side we bat-tle on-ward, vic-to-ry will come.

1. We meet today in freedom's cause
   And raise our voices high;
   We'll join our hands in union strong
   To battle or to die.

   CHORUS: Hold the fort for we are coming.
   Union men, be strong!
   Side by side we battle onward;
   Victory will come.

2. Look, my comrades, see the union
   Banners waving high.
   Reinforcements now appearing,
   Victory is nigh.

3. See our numbers still increasing;
   Hear the bugle blow.
   By our union we shall triumph
   Over every foe.

4. Fierce and long the battle rages
   But we will not fear.
   Help will come whene'er it's needed.
   Cheer, my comrades, cheer.

"Hold The Fort" is usually mentioned as the song of the British Transport Workers' Union, but its history is long and complicated.

The title comes from a famous incident of the American Civil War. In October, 1864, when Union troops were trapped in a fort at Allatoona Pass, near Atlanta, General Sherman sent a message which was signalled by flags from mountain to mountain: "General Sherman says hold fast. We are coming." Despite heavy attacks, the men held the fort until Sherman's army rescued them.

A certain Major Whittle, who had served with the Union forces, told this story at a Sunday School meeting in Rockford, Illinois, in May, 1870. In the audience was Philip P. Bliss, a well-known singing evangelist. Inspired by the story, that night Bliss wrote a gospel hymn with the following refrain:

"Hold the fort, for I am coming! Jesus signals still.
Wave the answer back to Heaven — 'By Thy Grace we will'."

Soon it was published in sheet music and became one of the songs used by Ira D. Sankey, the great evangelist and gospel singer. In 1873, he introduced it in Britain during a revival tour. It appeared as the first song in his collection of *Sacred Songs and Solos* which was published in London in 1875 as a result of requests for the songs he had popularized there. Toward the end of the nineteenth century it was parodied by the British Transport Workers who used it in their hard-fought fights for recognition.

Meanwhile, in the United States, the Knights of Labor had also realized the militant quality of the song. In the 1880's, when the Knights reached their peak of seven hundred thousand members, they were singing:

"Storm the fort, ye Knights of Labor,
Battle for your cause;
Equal rights for every neighbor,
Down with tyrant laws!"

This version may well have found its way to England where the Knights had a number of local assemblies, and influenced the Transport Workers when they came to write their own much better version. It in turn also crossed the Atlantic, getting back to the United States where the Wobblies took it up, and ever since it has been a standard union song.

WE SHALL NOT BE MOVED

2. We're fighting for our freedom; we shall not be moved.
   We're fighting for our freedom; we shall not be moved.
   Just like a tree that's planted by the water,
   We shall not be moved.

3. We're fighting for our children; we shall not be moved.

4. We'll build a mighty union; we shall not be moved.

5. .... is our leader; we shall not be moved.

Next to "Solidarity Forever," "We Shall Not Be Moved" is the best known and most widely sung labor song in the United States and Canada. Whenever union songs are heard, it is a must.

At convention hotels in the wee hours of the morning, enthusiastic union delegations have been heard singing "We Shall Not Be Moved" with great gusto, and, despite the determination expressed in the song, they have on occasion found themselves definitely "moved" — by hotel police.

The song is a great favorite on picket lines because it is easy to add dozens of verses telling the story of any particular strike. At one strike meeting in Biddeford, Maine, in 1945, several thousand textile workers roared it out, adding new verses continuously for a solid half hour.

"We Shall Not Be Moved" is based on the old gospel hymn, "I Shall Not Be Moved," which in turn was inspired by the verse from *Jeremiah*: "Blessed is the man that trusteth in the Lord for he shall be as a tree planted by the waters." It was first sung in 1931 by members of the West Virginia Miners' Union led by Frank Keeney, named in the original verse: "Frank Keeney is our captain, we shall not be moved."

Helen Norton Starr was working as a staff member of Brookwood Labor College when this song first appeared. She still remembers the first time she heard it:

"I remember the first time I heard 'We Shall Not Be Moved.' The only place that could be secured for the meeting in that particular valley was the front of a dilapidated Negro schoolhouse that stood in a depression among the hills — hills so green and tree-covered that only a sharp eye could see the scars of coal tipples. On the steps of the schoolhouse stood a mixed group of white and Negro miners and their wives, singing out their story and their hopes. The summer sun blazed down on them and on the miners' families seated on the slope in front. On the road above a group of state 'po-lice' and mine guards watched, their guns conspicuously displayed.

"That strike was lost and the Kanawha Valley was not unionized until 1933 under the NRA, but 'We Shall Not Be Moved' was sung all over the country and adapted to local conditions. I even saw one version put out by the Communists for tenant farmers which ran: 'Lenin is our leader, we shall not be moved'!"

In the South, workers normally sing "We Shall Not Be Moved" with great dignity, as though they were singing a hymn in church. In the North, it is sung with a powerful marching rhythm.

GREAT DAY

1. One of these mornings bright and fair
   We're going to build our union strong,
   Put on your wings and try the air,
   We're going to build our union strong.

CHORUS:
   Great day!
   Great day! The union's marching!
   Great day!
   We're going to build our union strong.

2. One of these mornings and it won't be long,
   We're going to build our union strong,
   Look for the scabs and they'll all be gone,
   We're going to build our union strong.

3. One of these mornings pretty darn soon,
   We're going to build our union strong,
   The boss will sing a different tune,
   We're going to build our union strong.

When the Negro slaves were freed in 1863, they sang many songs of rejoicing and jubilation:

   "This is the day of Jubilee,
   God's going to build up Zion's walls.
   The Lord has set his people free,
   God's going to build up Zion's walls.
   Great Day! Great day, the righteous marching!
   Great Day! God's going to build up Zion's walls!"

Some eighty-five years later a group of union members attending the Highlander Folk School in Monteagle, Tennessee, made up this fine union song using the same rousing tune.

OLD MA BELL

"Ma Bell" is the homey name the mammoth Bell Telephone Company likes to use when it is talking about itself. "Ma" was in trouble in 1947 when the Communications Workers of America called its members out on a nationwide strike against the Bell system. Out of the strike came this little ditty, sung to the tune of "The Old Gray Mare."

CASEY JONES

1. The workers on the S. P. Line to strike sent out a call,
   But Casey Jones, the engineer, he wouldn't strike at all.
   His boiler it was leaking, and its drivers on the bum,
   And his engine and its bearings they were all out of plumb.

   CHORUS: Casey Jones kept his junk pile running;
   Casey Jones was working double time;
   Casey Jones got a wooden medal
   For being good and faithful on the S. P. Line.

2. The workers said to Casey, "Won't you help us win this strike?"
   But Casey said, "Let me alone; you'd better take a hike."
   Then someone put a bunch of railroad ties across the track,
   And Casey hit the river with an awful crack.

   CHORUS: Casey Jones hit the river bottom;
   Casey Jones broke his blooming spine;
   Casey Jones was an Angeleno:
   He took a trip to Heaven on the S. P. Line.

3. When Casey Jones got up to Heaven to the Pearly Gate,
   He said, "I'm Casey Jones, the guy that pulled the S. P. freight."
   "You're just the man," said Peter, "Our musicians went on strike;
   You can get a job a-scabbing any time you like."

   CHORUS: Casey Jones got a job in Heaven;
   Casey Jones was doing mighty fine;
   Casey Jones went scabbing on the angels
   Just like he did to workers on the S. P. Line.

4. The angels got together and they said it wasn't fair
   For Casey Jones to go around a-scabbing everywhere.
   The Angels' Union No. 23, they sure were there,
   And they promptly fired Casey down the Golden Stair.

   CHORUS: Casey Jones went to Hell aflying.
   "Casey Jones!" the Devil said. "Oh, fine!
   Casey Jones, get busy shoveling sulphur —
   That's what you get for scabbing on the S. P. Line!"

Of the dozens of union songs written by Joe Hill, "Casey Jones" and "The Preacher and the Slave" are the only ones that have remained popular down to the present.

"Casey Jones" is said to have been written in 1911 when shopworkers on the Harriman System (which included the Southern Pacific Railroad — the S.P. Line) were on strike, and the engineers and other operating trades continued to run the trains. Joe Hill's verses were, of course, a parody of the original Casey Jones song about the "brave engineer" who died in the famous train wreck. Unfortunately copyright difficulties have made it impossible for the music to be included here.

Barrie Stavis, in his fascinating book about Hill, *The Man Who Never Died*, writes that with the publication of "Casey Jones" Joe Hill's writing career was launched: "It was sung by men on the picket line and by those who were clubbed and thrown into jail. It was printed on colored cards, about the size of a playing card, and sold, the proceeds going to the strike fund. Overnight the song became famous. Migratory laborers carried it on their lips as they moved across the nation; sailors carried it across the ocean."

ROLL THE UNION ON

With a steady beat

Words by JOHN HANDCOX and LEE HAYS

We're gon-na roll,—— we're gon-na roll,—— we're gon-na roll the u-nion on! We're gon-na roll,—— we're gon-na roll,—— we're gon-na roll the u-nion on! 1. If the boss is in the way we're gon-na roll it o-ver him, we're gon-na roll it o-ver him, we're gon-na roll it o-ver him. If the roll the u-nion on.

CHORUS: We're gonna roll, we're gonna roll,
We're gonna roll the union on!
We're gonna roll, we're gonna roll,
We're gonna roll the union on!

1. If the boss is in the way we're gonna roll it over him,
We're gonna roll it over him, we're gonna roll it over him.
If the boss is in the way we're gonna roll it over him;
We're gonna roll the union on!

2. If the scab is in the way we're gonna roll it over him,
We're gonna roll it over him, we're gonna roll it over him.
If the scab is in the way we're gonna roll it over him;
We're gonna roll the union on!

3. If the sheriff's in the way we're gonna roll it over him,
We're gonna roll it over him, we're gonna roll it over him.
If the sheriff's in the way we're gonna roll it over him,
We're gonna roll the union on!

4. Whoever's in the way we're gonna roll it over him,
We're gonna roll it over him, we're gonna roll it over him.
Whoever's in the way we're gonna roll it over him;
We're gonna roll the union on!

"Roll the Union On" is one of the most popular of all labor songs. It was long associated with the CIO's chief organizer, the colorful Allan Haywood, who died in 1953. Many union men remember how Haywood used to boom out "Roll the Union On" at conventions, meetings, and rallies.

The song was made up in 1936 at an Arkansas labor school and soon became popular with the Southern Tenant Farmers' Union. A Negro sharecropper and union organizer called John Handcox gets credit for the first verse, and Lee Hays added others. Like so many good union songs it is based on a gospel hymn: "Roll the Chariot On." A few quick changes, and the gospel song became a union song. Thus, starting with the original words:

"If the Devil's in the way
We're going to roll it over him,
We're going to roll the chariot on,"

it was easy to substitute "Boss" for "Devil" and "union" for "chariot" — and another union song was born.

THE SCABS CRAWL IN

The scabs crawl in, the scabs crawl out,
They crawl in under and all about.
They crawl in early, they crawl in late,
They crawl in under the factory gate.

"Scab" is the ugliest name a union man can hurl at a fellow worker. The term, which archaically meant "a mean, dirty fellow," is applied by trade unionists to workers who refuse to join a strike or a union, and especially to those who take a striker's job. In Britain, the corresponding term is "blackleg"; in France, it is "jaune," or yellow.

Scabs have been called many things by many people, but Jack London's description dwarfs all others:

"After God had finished the rattlesnake, the toad, the vampire, He had some awful substance left with which he made a scab.

"When a scab comes down the street, men turn their backs and angels weep in Heaven, and the Devil shuts the gates of Hell to keep him out.

"Esau sold his birthright for a mess of pottage. Judas Iscariot sold his Savior for thirty pieces of silver. Benedict Arnold sold his country for a promise of a commission in the British Army. The modern strikebreaker sells his birthright, his country, his wife, his children, and his fellow men for an unfilled promise from his employer, trust, or corporation."

This little ditty, to the familiar tune of "The Worms Crawl In," was popular on the picket line of the Western Union strike in New York in 1946.

DOWN IN A COAL MINE

Words and music by
J. B. GEOGHEGAN

I am a jo-vial col-lier lad, as blithe as blithe can be, And let the times be good or bad, they're all the same to me; There's lit-tle of this world I know and care less for its ways, For where the dog star ne-ver glows, I wear a-way the days.

(over)

CHORUS

Down in a coal mine, un-der-neath the ground, Where a gleam of sun-shine ne-ver can be found; Dig-ging dus-ky dia-monds all the year a-round, Down in a coal mine un-der-neath the ground.

1. I am a jovial collier lad, as blithe as blithe can be,
   And let the times be good or bad, they're all the same to me;
   It's little of the world I know and care less for its ways,
   For where the Dog Star never glows I wear away my days.

CHORUS: Down in a coal mine, underneath the ground,
                Where a gleam of sunshine never can be found;
                Digging dusky diamonds all the year around,
                Down in a coal mine, underneath the ground.

2. My hands are horny, hard, and black from working in the vein,
   And, like the clothes upon my back, my speech is rough and plain;
   Well, if I stumble with my tongue, I've one excuse to say:
   It's not the collier's heart that's bad, it's his head that goes astray.

3. At every shift, be it soon or late, I haste my bread to earn,
And anxiously my kindred wait and watch for my return;
For death that levels all alike, whate'er their rank may be,
Amid the fire and damp may strike and fling his darts at me.

4. How little do the great ones care, who sit at home secure,
What hidden dangers colliers dare, what hardships they endure;
The very fires their mansions boast, to cheer themselves and wives,
Mayhap were kindled at the cost of jovial colliers' lives.

5. Then cheer up, lads, and make ye much of every joy you can;
But let your mirth be always such as best becomes a man;
However fortune turns about we'll still be jovial souls;
What would this country be without the lads that look for coals?

"Down in a Coal Mine" was originally a stage song, written by the American comedian, J. B. Geohegan, in 1872. It was soon adopted by the coal miners and became the best known of all miners' songs, particularly in the anthracite fields of Pennsylvania. It also crossed over to Britain where it became widely popular and is still sung today. There the tune is usually changed to that of the old Irish song, "The Roving Journeyman."

DARK AS A DUNGEON

Words and music by
MERLE TRAVIS

(over)

50

1. Come all you young fellows so young and so fine,
Seek not your fortune in the dark dreary mine.
It will form like a habit and seep in your soul
Till the stream of your blood is as black as the coal.

CHORUS: It's dark as a dungeon, and damp as the dew;
The dangers are many, and the pleasures are few,
Where the rain never falls and the sun never shines —
It's dark as a dungeon, way down in the mines.

2. There's many a man I have known in my day
Who lived just to labor his whole life away;
Like a fiend for his dope and a drunkard his wine,
A man will have lust for the lure of the mine.

3. I hope when I'm gone and the ages will roll,
My body will blacken and turn into coal;
Then I'll look from the door of my heavenly home
And pity the miner a-digging my bones.

Merle Travis, who wrote "Dark as a Dungeon" as well as the better-known "Sixteen Tons," was the son of a hard-working coal-miner of Beech Creek, Kentucky. While he himself never worked in the mines, the hardships and struggle of the miner's life were burned into his consciousness and he never forgot them.

Many years after he left the Kentucky coal fields to win fame in Hollywood as a singer and song-writer, he could still recall with emotion the bleak conditions under which the coal miner's family lived. In the *United Mineworkers' Journal* he wrote:

"I have known the fruits of strikes. The bitter and the sweet. Hunger and music . . . Who deserves more credit than the wife of a coal miner? Mother was one. She never complained about the hardships that were hers in abundance. Lighting the coal-oil lamp long before daylight, and cooking breakfast for her children and husband.

"Taylor, my oldest brother, would come home and get 'washed up.' How well I remember the galvanized tub set in the middle of the floor — the big black pot of water poured in — the steam — and then enough cold water to make it just right. When I'd watch him wash the black coal dust from a little rose tattoo on his arm I longed for the day when I could work in the mine and have a tattoo . . . He practically broke every rib in his body in a mine accident and it changed his whole life . . ."

In 1947, Travis recorded an album called "Folk Songs of the Hills," including several songs he had written about the miners he knew so well. In "Dark as a Dungeon" he manages to express the peculiar isolation of the miner's lot. No other song portrays so well the loneliness, the constant presence of danger and potential death, and the strange attraction which keeps a man working "way down in the mines."

SIXTEEN TONS

Words and music by
MERLE TRAVIS

With a driving beat

Now some peo-ple say a man's made out of mud, But a poor man's made out of mus-cle and blood, Mus-cle and blood, skin and bone, A mind that's weak and a back that's strong. You load Six-teen tons and what do you get? You get a-no-ther day ol-der and dee-per in debt. Saint

Pe-ter, don't you call me 'cause I can't go, I owe my soul to the com-pa-ny store.

2. Well, com-pa-ny store.

2. I was born one morning when the sun didn't shine,
I picked up my shovel and I walked to the mine.
I loaded sixteen tons of number nine coal,
And the straw boss hollered, "Well, bless my soul!"

3. I was born one morning in the drizzling rain;
Fighting and trouble is my middle name.
I was raised in the bottoms by a momma hound —
I'm mean as a dog but I'm gentle as a lamb.

4. If you see me coming, you better step aside;
A lot of men didn't, and a lot of men died.
I got a fist of iron and a fist of steel,
If the right one don't get you then the left one will.

Another fine mining song by Merle Travis is "Sixteen Tons" which was written at the same time as "Dark as a Dungeon." The key line, "I owe my soul to the company store," was a favorite expression of Travis's father who worked in the coal mines of Beech Creek, Kentucky. Travis said:

"My Dad never saw real money. He was constantly in debt to the coal company. When shopping was needed, Dad would go to a window and draw little brass tokens against his account. They could only be spent at the company store. He used to say: 'I can't afford to die. I owe my soul to the company store.'

"There were two coal mines in Beech Creek. One was called No. 5, the other No. 9. You were lucky if you worked in No. 5 because No. 9 had a low ceiling which made it harder to dig your daily quota of sixteen tons."

An interesting postscript: Eight years after Merle Travis first recorded "Sixteen Tons" it was recorded by "Tennessee Ernie" Ford and quickly became a phenomenal hit. More than a million records were sold in a shorter time than any previous recording, and it stayed on the top of the Hit Parade for months. It was the first song of its type to achieve such universal popularity. Some attributed its success to the fine driving beat achieved in Ford's record; others say the song strikes home because so many of us live on credit and owe our souls to some sort of company store.

WHICH SIDE ARE YOU ON?

Words by FLORENCE REECE

Come all of you good wor - kers, good news to you I'll tell of

how the good old u - nion has come in here to dwell.

CHORUS

Which side are you on? Which side are you on?

Which side are you on? Which side are you on?

1. Come all of you good workers,
   Good news to you I'll tell
   Of how the good old union
   Has come in here to dwell.

CHORUS: Which side are you on?
        Which side are you on?
        Which side are you on?
        Which side are you on?

2. My daddy was a miner
   And I'm a miner's son,
   And I'll stick with the union
   Till ev'ry battle's won.

3. They say in Harlan County
   There are no neutrals there;
   You'll either be a union man
   Or a thug for J. H. Blair.

4. Oh, workers, can you stand it?
   Oh, tell me how you can.
   Will you be a lousy seab
   Or will you be a man?

5. Don't scab for the bosses,
   Don't listen to their lies.
   Us poor folks haven't got a chance
   Unless we organize.

The bloodiest battles to build a union have been in the coal fields — in Pennsylvania, West Virginia, Illinois, Colorado, and Kentucky. And surely the toughest and meanest of all the coal fields where men fought for a voice and a place in the sun was "Bloody Harlan" in Kentucky.

The "Harlan County Blues" summed up the story:

> "You didn't have to be a drunk to get throwed in the can.
> The only thing you needed be was just a union man."

In 1931, coal miners in Harlan County were on strike. Armed company deputies roamed the countryside, terrorizing the mining communities, looking for union leaders to beat, jail, or kill. But coal miners, brought up lean and hard in the Kentucky mountain country, knew how to fight back, and heads were bashed and bullets fired on both sides in Bloody Harlan.

It was this kind of class war — the mine owners and their hired deputies on the one side, and the independent, free-wheeling Kentucky coal-miners on the other — that provided the climate for Florence Reece's fine song, "Which Side Are You On?" In it she captured the spirit of her times with blunt eloquence.

Mrs. Reece wrote from personal experience. Her husband, Sam, was one of the union leaders, and Sheriff J. H. Blair and his men came to her house in search of him when she was alone with her seven children. They ransacked the whole house and then kept watch outside, ready to shoot Sam down if he returned.

One day during this tense period Mrs. Reece tore a sheet from a wall calendar and wrote the words to "Which Side Are You On?" The simple form of the song made it easy to adapt for use in other strikes, and many different versions have circulated.

The tune is usually said to be an old Baptist hymn, "Lay the Lily Low," but the British folklorist, A. L. Lloyd, points out its similarity to that of the British ballad, "Jack Munro," which uses "Lay the Lily Low" as a refrain.

WEST VIRGINIA HILLS

Music by H. E. ENGLE
Words by WALTER SEACRIST

There's a u-nion in the West Vir-gi-nia hills! Tho' o'er scab fields I should roam, Still I'll dream of hap-py home, and the Rednecks in the West Vir-gi-nia Hills. 2. Oh, those Hills.

This song was written in the West Virginia coal fields in the early 1930's. It first appeared in one of the earliest collections of labor songs, which was put out by Brookwood Labor College.

While "West Virginia Hills" is not generally known in the labor movement, it evokes great emotion when sung to a group of workers and deserves broader recognition.

Agnes Douty, who was in West Virginia in the 'thirties conducting a recreation program for the miners' children, was the first person to sing the song in union circles outside its native state. She recalls the atmosphere in which the song was written:

"I heard this song first in West Virginia in the summer of '32 or '33 during the revolt of the West Virginia miners against John L. Lewis. The union had refused to accept the terms of the contract that Lewis had signed for them and carried on their strike without official sanction or support. They were all evicted and lived in tent colonies for about one and a half years.

" 'West Virginia Hills' was sung to the tune of the state anthem with words supplied by a handsome preacher-miner named Walter Seacrist. Seacrist was more or less the official balladeer of the union. The song was universally sung by the evicted miners."

58

THE DEATH OF MOTHER JONES

Reminiscently

The world to-day is mourn-ing —— the death of Mo - ther
Jones; —————— Grief and sor - row ho - ver
a - round the mi - ners' homes. ————— This grand old cham-pion of
la - bor ————— has gone to a bet - ter land, ——— But the hard -

work - ing mi - ners, ——— they miss her guid - ing hand. ——

2. Through the hills and over the valleys in every mining town,
   Mother Jones was ready to help them; she never let them down.
   In front with the striking miners she always could be found;
   She fought for right and justice; she took a noble stand.

3. With a spirit strong and fearless, she hated that which was wrong;
   She never gave up fighting until her breath was gone.
   May the workers all get together to carry out her plan,
   And bring back better conditions for every laboring man.

Mary ("Mother") Jones was the most remarkable woman produced by the American labor movement. She was born in 1830 and lived for a full hundred years. She spent fifty of those years fighting fiercely on behalf of her "children": the coal miners and the rest of the working class.

Her own four children and her husband — a staunch member of the Iron Moulders Union — all died during a yellow fever epidemic in 1867, and a few years later Mother Jones became active in the Knights of Labor. She soon won recognition as a fiery speaker, a fearless agitator and organizer, and a great strike strategist. She could not be frightened away by company thugs or state militia. She was threatened with jail — and many times the threats were kept — but she was never intimidated.

"Mother Jones, we need you to win this strike." That was all she needed to send her rushing off to West Virginia or Colorado, Pennsylvania or Alabama. She participated in great railway strikes. She helped the textile workers fight against child labor. At the age of eighty-nine she fought vigorously during the great steel strike of 1919.

But the greatest part of her fighting days she spent with her beloved miners. She shared their shacks and their bit of food in the dreary mine patches. She organized bands of women and marched with them for miles through the hills to help unionize the scab mines. She inspired the men with her burning eloquence, her absolute fearlessness, and her never-wavering devotion. And sometimes she helped bury miners' little children who died for lack of milk.

In her autobiography Mother Jones wrote:

> "The story of coal is always the same. It is a dark story. For a second's more sun-light, men must fight like tigers. For the privilege of seeing the color of their children's eyes by the light of the sun, fathers must fight as beasts in the jungle. That life may have something of decency, something of beauty — a picture, a new dress, a bit of cheap lace fluttering in the window — for this, men who work down in the mines must struggle and lose, struggle and win."

Mother Jones died in 1930, only a few short years before the hundred thousand coal miners in West Virginia became solidly organized. Soon afterwards "The Death of Mother Jones" began to circulate. Agnes Douty heard it in West Virginia in 1932 when she was working there with coal-miners' children. Mark Starr, Education Director of the International Ladies' Garment Workers' Union, heard Walter Seacrist, author of "The West Virginia Hills," sing it in the early 'thirties. No one is sure where it came from, but it could have been written by any one of the thousands of "children" whom Mother Jones loved and fought for all her life.

THE BLANTYRE EXPLOSION

By Clyde's bon-ny banks where I sad-ly did wan-der, a-mong the pit-heaps as the eve-ning drew nigh, I spied a fair mai-den all dressed in deep mourn-ing, A-weep-ing and wail-ing, with ma-ny a sigh.

1. sigh.

2. I sigh.

BY PERMISSION OF A. L. LLOYD.

1. By Clyde's bonny banks where I sadly did wander,
   Among the pit-heaps as the evening drew nigh,
   I spied a fair maiden all dressed in deep mourning,
   A-weeping and wailing with many a sigh.

2. I stepped up beside her and thus I addressed her:
   "Pray tell me, fair maid, of your trouble and pain."
   Sobbing and sighing, at last she did answer:
   "Johnny Murphy, kind sir, was my true lover's name.

3. "Twenty-one years of age, full of youth and good-looking,
   To work down the mines from High Blantyre he came.
   The wedding was fixed, all the guests were invited
   That calm summer evening young Johnny was slain.

4. "The explosion was heard; all the women and children
   With pale anxious faces they haste to the mine.
   When the truth was made known, the hills rang with their moaning.
   Three hundred and ten young miners were slain."

5. Now husbands and wives and sweethearts and brothers,
   That Blantyre explosion they'll never forget.
   And all you young miners that hear my sad story,
   Shed a tear for the victims who're laid to their rest.

Mining is the most hazardous of all occupations. In his book, *John L. Lewis*, Saul Alinsky writes:

"The miner is never alone, for death is all about him. It is over his head with the collapsing roof and his sudden crushing burial; it is in front of him in the pockets of invisible, odorless, tasteless, deadly methane gas released by cutting into the coal face and ignited by his explosives. Then it comes as a blinding flash and oblivion. It is behind him in the long tunnels, where it comes with the reptilian hiss of the rolling wall of smoke and flames as he shakes and screams in agony knowing that death is coming either by cremation or asphyxiation.

"He knows the toll of his underground fraternity, for every morning he goes down under with the odds just a shade more than nine to one in his favor of escaping death or injury. Every day he shoots dice with death. Compare his mortality rate with that of the armed services. The miner knows that he digs death as well as coal, and the death tonnage is appalling.

"He knew some of the 68,842 miners killed from 1910 through 1945, and he knew some of the 2,275,000 injured. He had stood awkward and choked with emotion before some of the 211,468 widows and orphans of these men. He contributed generously to collections for the impoverished survivors with the chilled feeling that the next collection might be for his widow and children."

A. L. Lloyd, the British folk-song authority who published a collection of coal-mining songs called *Come All Ye Bold Miners*, says:

"Probably the larger part of mining balladry is concerned with disasters. At one time these ballads were often made by the writers of street-songs, who put the sensational news of the day into broadsheet verse; but many miners have been moved by the drama and horror of a pit explosion to make up commemorative songs. After the eighteen-forties, the standard form for pit-disaster ballads came to be the alternative eight and six-syllable phrases of the Irish street-song, the 'come-all-ye,' a style of ballad which has proved more adaptable than any other for the requirements of industrial folksong. Many an old miner preserves the saga of some mine disaster that has faded even from local memory."

A good example is this ballad, which describes the explosion at Dixon's Colliery, High Blantyre, near Glasgow, on October 22, 1877, in which over two hundred miners were killed. It is one of the few British mine disaster ballads that has been collected in America (see *Pennsylvania Songs and Legends*, p. 44). Its form is closer to that of the elegy than the "come-all-ye"; the melody has been used for several other songs including the lumberjack favorite, "The Lost Jimmie Whalen," and the American Civil War ballad, "The Cumberland's Crew." It is also closely related to the cowboy song, "The Streets of Laredo."

UNION MAN

Words by ALBERT MORGAN

I think I sing this lit - tle song, Hope I say it no - thing wrong,

Hope my song she bring good cheer, Just like cou-ple of shots of beer.

CHORUS

U - nion man! U - nion man! He must have full din - ner can!

A. F. L., C. I. O., cal - lin' strike, out she go.

1. I think I sing this little song,
   Hope I say it nothing wrong,
   Hope my song she bring good cheer
   Just like couple of shots of beer.

CHORUS: Union man! Union man!
         He must have full dinner can!
         AFL, CIO
         Callin' strike, out she go!

2. We all got contract, she expire;
   Mr. Lewis mad like fire;
   Miners strikin' too much time,
   Uncle Sam take over mine.

3. We signin' contract, we get raise
   After strikin' twenty days.
   Butcher comes and ringin' bell
   He raises prices—what the hell!

4. I'm drinkin' too much beer last night,
   To go to work I don't feel right.
   In my can some bread and meat,
   I'm too dam' sick, I cannot eat.

5. I fire shot at ten o'clock,
   Tumble brushes full of rock,
   Timber breakin' o'er my head,
   Jeepers cripes I think I'm dead!

This is one of the many mining songs George Korson collected for the Library of Congress. Albert Morgan, the man who composed it, sang it for him in the Newkirk Tunnel Mine in Pennsylvania in 1946. Korson commented: "This short ditty is an excellent example of the way the folk reflect in their songs the varied phases of their life. Better than an economist's report, the five stanzas are a satiric comment on rising wages and rising prices." Its light-hearted approach is in sharp contrast to the other miners' songs, which date from earlier and grimmer times.

"Mr. Lewis" in the second verse is, of course, John L. Lewis, the long-time president of the United Mine Workers of America, and the reference to "Uncle Sam" recalls the miners' strikes during World War II when the U. S. Government intervened and ordered the miners back to work.

MY SWEETHEART'S THE MULE IN THE MINES

Before the mines were electrified, every colliery kept a stable full of mules to haul its coal cars. The mules were driven by boys about twelve to fifteen years old. George Korson gives this account:

"A boy had to be down in the mine before seven, get his mule out of the stable, bring it to the foot of the shaft or slope and hitch it to a trip of empty cars. He hopped on the first car, cracked his long braided leather whip and shouted. When he sang, the ditty probably was 'My Sweetheart's the Mule in the Mines,' many ribald versions of which echoed through the mines . . . A boy had to learn not only to drive a mule without reins but to govern it with his voice. He had stock cues, but they were not effective unless seasoned with oaths and peppery English."

The driver boys' ditty was based on a popular song of the 1890's called "My Sweetheart's the Man in the Moon."

A MINER'S LIFE

Resolutely

Mi - ner's life is like a sai - lor's 'Board a
rocks, they're fall-ing dai - ly; Care-less

ship to cross the wave; Ev - 'ry day
mi ners al - ways fail. Keep your hand

his life's in dan - ger, still he ven - tures, be-ing
u - pon the dol - lar,

brave. Watch the
And your eye u - pon the

(over)

CHORUS

1. A miner's life is like a sailor's
   'Board a ship to cross the wave;
   Ev'ry day his life's in danger;
   Still he ventures, being brave,
   Watch the rocks, they're falling daily;
   Careless miners always fail:
   Keep your hand upon the dollar,
   And your eye upon the scale!

2. Soon this trouble will be ended;
   Union men will have their rights,
   After many years of bondage,
   Digging days and digging nights.
   Then by honest weight we'll labor;
   Union workers never fail:
   Keep your hand upon the dollar,
   And your eye upon the scale!

CHORUS: Union miners, stand together!
Heed no operator's tale!
Keep your hand upon the dollar,
And your eye upon the scale!

3. You've been docked and docked again, boys;
   You've been loading two for one.
   What have you to show for working
   Since this mining has begun?
   Worn-out boots and worn-out miners,
   And your children growing pale:
   Keep your hand upon the dollar,
   And your eye upon the scale!

4. In conclusion, bear in mem'ry,
   Keep this password in your mind:
   God provides for ev'ry worker
   When in union they combine.
   Stand like men, and linked together
   Vict'ry for you will prevail:
   Keep your hand upon the dollar,
   And your eye upon the scale!

This song is sung by miners in Wales and Nova Scotia as well as in the United States. George Korson was the first to record it: in Mt. Hope, West Virginia, in 1940 when he was collecting material for his book, *Coal Dust on the Fiddle*. He calls it "Miner's Lifeguard," and dates it as "1900-1910."

In Britain, A. L. Lloyd heard the same song in Aberaman, South Wales, and published it in his book, *Come All Ye Bold Miners*. He suggests that either it was a song of Welsh origin exported to America or that it evolved among Welsh migrant miners in the United States because it is sung to the Welsh hymn tune "Calon Lan."

However, in the States this tune was used for a nineteenth-century sacred song called "Life's Railway to Heaven," and the union song began as a parody of this:

"Round the bend and through the tunnel,
Never falter, never fail;
Keep your hand upon the throttle,
And your eye upon the rail."

The same hymn also inspired the textile workers to create a song beginning:

"A weaver's life is like an engine
Coming round the mountain steep."

The oft-repeated warning in the chorus to "keep your eye upon the scale" refers to the coal owners' practice of underweighing the miners' coal cars before the unions succeeded in appointing a union checkweighman.

HARD TIMES IN THE MILL

Plaintively

Ev-'ry morn-ing at half-past four you hear the cooks hop on the floor.

CHORUS

It's hard times in the mill, my love, hard times in the mill.

1. Every morning at half-past four
   You hear the cooks hop on the floor.

CHORUS: It's hard times in the mill, my love,
   Hard times in the mill.

2. Every morning just at five
   You gotta get up, dead or alive.

3. Every morning at six o'clock
   Two cold biscuits, hard as a rock.

4. Every morning at half-past nine
   The bosses are cussin' and the spinners are cryin'.

5. They docked me a nickel, they docked me a dime,
   They sent me to the office to get my time.

6. Cotton mill boys don't make enough
   To buy them tobacco and a box of snuff.

7. Every night when I get home,
   A piece of corn bread and an old jawbone.

8. Ain't it enough to break your heart?
   Hafta work all day and at night it's dark.

In 1791, Samuel Slater, the "Father of Cotton Manufacture in America," picked out a choice water site in Pawtucket, Rhode Island, and established the first textile mill on the North American continent. And ever since — with only rare and periodic exceptions — it's been "hard times in the mill" for the men and women (and children) — the carders, spinners, weavers, dyers, and finishers — in the textile industry.

The huge, sprawling textile industry has a long, unhappy history of low wages, long hours, child labor, stretch-out and speed-up, company-dominated mill towns, chronic unemployment and instability. Many factors have contributed to the sickness of the textile industry: cut-throat competition from thousands of small mills; backward family managements who let mills and machinery get run-down and out-of-date; an overly complex and inefficient sales and distribution set-up; large-scale migration from New England to the South; over-expansion during wars; competition from low-wage textile industries overseas and new plastic industries at home — the accumulation of 165 years of ills and troubles.

During the past century and a half, literally thousands of strikes and revolts have flared up as textile workers struggled for a better life for themselves and their families. One hundred and forty years after Slater opened his mill working young children (some only seven years old) twelve hours a day, southern textile workers were still fighting child labor and striking against the twelve-hour day.

Fall River, New Bedford, Lawrence, Passaic, Paterson, Danville, Marion, Gastonia, and other great textile centers have had their struggles, their heroes, and their martyrs. In the unsuccessful 1934 general strike when 400,000 workers walked out of mills in hundreds of communities, twenty workers were killed and 25,000 blacklisted.

Even in recent years, when most manufacturing industries have become well organized and workers have improved their standard of living, it is still "hard times in the mill" for the average textile worker. While the twelve-hour day and child labor have been abolished, low wages and chronic unemployment still persist. Long established factories go out of business regularly, throwing thousands of older workers on the street. And always there is the unyielding opposition of most textile employers to union organization. In the great southern textile industry only one out of ten workers is organized, and company opposition has included outright firing of union sympathizers, intimidation and threats to union members, denial of the use of meeting halls or newspaper advertising space to the union, refusal to bargain, shutting down of the mill after the union won the election.

"Hard Times in the Mill," an adaptation of the familiar "Hard Times in Cryderville Jail," was written by workers in the Columbia Duck Mills, Columbia, South Carolina, at the beginning of this century. These verses were supplied by Margaret (Pat) Knight and Norris Tibbetts who got them from southern textile workers when they were working for the Textile Workers' Union of America in the 1940's.

BREAD AND ROSES

Music by CAROLINE KOHLSAAT
Words by JAMES OPPENHEIM

As we come march-ing, march-ing, in the beau-ty of the day, A

mil- lion dar-kened kit- chens, a thou-sand mill lofts gray, Are

touched with all the ra- diance that a sud-den sun dis- clo- ses, For the

peo- ple hear us sing - ing, "Bread and ro - ses, Bread and ro - ses."

1. As we come marching, marching in the beauty of the day,
   A million darkened kitchens, a thousand mill lofts gray,
   Are touched with all the radiance that a sudden sun discloses,
   For the people hear us singing: "Bread and roses! Bread and roses!"

2. As we come marching, marching, we battle too for men,
   For they are women's children, and we mother them again.
   Our lives shall not be sweated from birth until life closes;
   Hearts starve as well as bodies; give us bread, but give us roses!

3. As we come marching, marching, unnumbered women dead
   Go crying through our singing their ancient cry for bread.
   Small art and love and beauty their drudging spirits knew.
   Yes, it is bread we fight for—but we fight for roses, too!

4. As we come marching, marching, we bring the greater days.
   The rising of the women means the rising of the race.
   No more the drudge and idler—ten that toil where one reposes,
   But a sharing of life's glories: Bread and roses! Bread and roses!

In 1912, in the great woolen center of Lawrence, Massachusetts, 20,000 workers walked out of the mills in spontaneous protest against a cut in their weekly pay. Workers had been averaging $8.76 for a 56-hour work week when a state law made 54 hours the maximum for women and for minors under 18. The companies reduced all hours to 54 but refused to raise wage rates to make up for the average loss of 31¢ per week suffered by each worker because of the reduction in hours.

This caused the walkout which rocked the great New England textile industry. Under the aggressive leadership of the Industrial Workers of the World the strike became front-page news throughout the country. This is how IWW leader Bill Haywood described the Lawrence strike in his autobiography, *Bill Haywood's Book*:

> "It was a wonderful strike, the most significant strike, the greatest strike that has ever been carried on in this country or any other country. And the most significant part of that strike was that it was a democracy. The strikers had a committee of 56, representing 27 different languages. The boss would have to see all the committee to do any business with them. And immediately behind that committee was a substitute committee of another 56 prepared in the event of the original committee's being arrested. Every official in touch with affairs at Lawrence had a substitute selected to take his place in the event of being thrown in jail."

After ten weeks the strikers won important concessions from the woolen companies, not only for themselves but also for 250,000 textile workers throughout New England.

During one of the many parades conducted by the strikers some young girls carried a banner with the slogan: "We want bread and roses too." This inspired James Oppenheim to write his poem, "Bread and Roses," which was set to music by Caroline Kohlsaat.

There is also an Italian song with the same title, "Pan e Rose," written by the Italian-American poet Arturo Giovannitti which is used by the Italian Dressmakers' Local 89 of the International Ladies' Garment Workers' Union.

WE ARE BUILDING A STRONG UNION

1. We are building a strong union,
   We are building a strong union,
   We are building a strong union,
   Workers in the mill!

2. Every member makes us stronger,
   Every member makes us stronger,
   Every member makes us stronger,
   Workers in the mill!

3. We won't budge until we conquer,
   We won't budge until we conquer,
   We won't budge until we conquer,
        Workers in the mill!

4. We shall rise and gain our freedom,
   We shall rise and gain our freedom,
   We shall rise and gain our freedom,
        Workers in the mill!

5. We are building a strong union,
   We are building a strong union,
   We are building a strong union,
        Workers in the mill!

A strike can be tragic and glorious, bitter and beautiful. A strike can bring out all the qualities of courage and fear, love and hate, that lie buried deep in a man's soul. Such a strike took place in the little town of Marion, North Carolina, in 1929, and out of this strike came one of the most powerful of all union songs: "We Are Building A Strong Union."

Marion, North Carolina, lies at the base of the beautiful Blue Ridge Mountains. The colorful background of this "land of the sky" contrasted sharply with the drab mill villages, with their houses standing on high brick stilts, with their outdoor privies. The villages had no sewers and no running water. Wages averaged about ten dollars a week for 72 hours. When twenty minutes per day was added to the 12-hour shift, the workers revolted.

In his book, *When Southern Labor Stirs,* Tom Tippett captured the spirit of the cotton mill workers:

"The people were expressing the sensation of industrial freedom for the first time in their lives. Hymns from their churches were sung at the strike meetings and were later transcribed into songs of the strike. Religious emotions, too, were transferred into the struggle. A striker would rise to speak, and in his zeal for the brotherhood of unionism he used the very terms of a church revival meeting. The crowd would encourage him with 'amen.' Thus everybody would envisage a new kind of religion and a new kind of enemy. Many a prayer went up that summer asking God Almighty to 'help us drive the cotton mill devil out of this here village.'

" . . . Everybody who participated in the early part of the Marion strike will remember those days — the picket lines at night with their camp-fires burning; the women and men stationed there chanting rewritten Negro spirituals across the darkness to inspire faith and courage; the mass meetings oftentimes in a downpour of rain, and the strikers singing. In those early weeks of the strike the Marion cotton-mill workers caught a glimpse of something intangible, but something which they obviously and unanimously felt none the less . . . The strike was a new experience. It was the first time many of the workers had ever thought of themselves as anything but mill 'hands'."

The strike ended in tragedy and bloodshed when the state militia killed six workers and wounded twenty-five others. All were shot in the back while running from gunfire. The union was smashed, but one thing remains: this fine song which inspired the workers in their struggle.

"We Are Building A Strong Union" is based on the old hymn, "We Are Climbing Jacob's Ladder." It was also adapted by coal miners who sang: "We have toiled through dark and danger, workers in the mine!"

THE WINNSBORO COTTON MILL BLUES

Old man Sar-gent, sit-ting at the desk, the damn' old fool won't give us a rest.

He'd take the nic-kels off a dead man's eyes to buy Co-ca Co-la and

Es-ki-mo pies. I got the blues, I got the blues, I got the

Winns-bo-ro cot-ton mill blues. ———— Lor-dy, Lor-dy,

2. When I die, don't bury me at all,
   Just hang me up on the spool-room wall;
   Place a knotter in my hand,
   So I can spool in the Promised Land.

3. When I die, don't bury me deep,
   Bury me down on Six Hundred Street;
   Place a bobbin in each hand
   So I can doff in the Promised Land.

This vivid cotton-mill song was recorded by Bill Wolff in 1939 when he was teaching a summer course at the Southern School for Workers in North Carolina. A woman in the group came up and sang it for him; the record is now in the Library of Congress. It has since been recorded by the fine banjo-player and folksinger, Peter Seeger.

A spool is a reel for winding yarn; a knotter is a little gadget used for tying the ends of the yarn together; a doffer is a worker who takes filled bobbins from the spinning frames.

THE MILL WAS MADE OF MARBLE

Words and music by JOE GLAZER

made out of gold, _____ And no - bo - dy e - ver got tired, and no - bo - dy e - ver grew old. _____

1. I dreamed that I had died
   And gone to my reward—
   A job in Heaven's textile plant
   On a golden boulevard.

CHORUS:
   The mill was made of marble,
   The machines were made out of gold,
   And nobody ever got tired,
   And nobody ever grew old.

2. This mill was built in a garden—
   No dust or lint could be found.
   The air was so fresh and so fragrant
   With flowers and trees all around.

3. It was quiet and peaceful in heaven—
   There was no clatter or boom.
   You could hear the most beautiful music
   As you worked at the spindle and loom.

4. There was no unemployment in heaven;
   We worked steady all through the year;
   We always had food for the children;
   We never were haunted by fear.

5. When I woke from this dream about heaven
   I wondered if some day there'd be
   A mill like that one down below here
     on earth
   For workers like you and like me.

In Rockingham, North Carolina, at the Safie Textile Mill, members of the Textile Workers Union of America, CIO, went on strike on April 17, 1947, to get a minimum wage of sixty-five cents an hour.

After five months on the picket line the strike was lost and the union broken. This was one of many long and bitter strikes fought by textile workers in the South against the unbending opposition of the mill owners.

One day an old striker brought Margaret (Pat) Knight, a member of the Textile Workers' staff, a tattered sheet of paper containing eight lines about a "mill built of marble." Pat Knight showed these words to Joe Glazer, who reworked it, set it to music, and added four verses, turning it into the song known today as "The Mill Was Made of Marble."

This has become one of the most popular union songs of the last twenty-five years, and was a favorite of the late CIO President, Philip Murray.

ANTHEM OF THE ILGWU

rise in our might, with the I - L - G - W - U!

1. One battle is won, but the fight's just begun,
   And the union flag's unfurled;
   United we're strong, let us march toward the dawn
   Of a brave new workers' world.

CHORUS: Oh, Union of the Garment Workers,
         To you we ever will be true;
         We'll build and we'll fight, and we'll rise in our **might**
         With the I.L.G.W.U.!

2. North, south, east, and west, all the workers oppressed.
   Join the Union ranks today;
   Our banners are bright as they float red and white
   Where our union leads the way.

The International Ladies' Garment Workers' Union, established in 1900, is one of America's oldest and best-known unions. The ILGWU has pioneered in many fields, including that of union songs. It began publishing its own union song book in 1935 and to date has distributed 50,000 copies of half a dozen editions.

The 1951 edition of the ILGWU song book, called "Everybody Sings," contains no less than thirty garment workers' songs. In the introduction, Education Director Mark Starr writes: "These songs mock our foes, commemorate our martyrs, and hymn faith in our union, in democracy, our country, and in the international solidarity of free trade unions everywhere. Their inspiration, satire, and sentiment arise directly out of the workers' struggles. Such songs are part of the real folk music of modern America."

The ILGWU made musical history in 1938 when its own musical comedy, "Pins and Needles," opened on Broadway and played for two years. It has also made one of the best labor movies, "With These Hands," which opens to the strains of the "ILGWU Anthem." Written in 1934, this song is a favorite of the various choruses sponsored by the union throughout the country.

TAKE THIS HAMMER

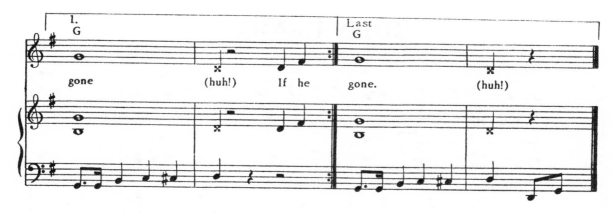

1. Take this hammer, (huh!) carry it to the captain, (huh!)
   Take this hammer, (huh!) carry it to the captain, (huh!)
   Take this hammer, (huh!) carry it to the captain, (huh!)
   Tell him I'm gone, (huh!) tell him I'm gone. (huh!)

2. If he asks you, (huh!) was I running, (huh!)
   If he asks you, (huh!) was I running, (huh!)
   If he asks you, (huh!) was I running, (huh!)
   Tell him I was flying, (huh!) tell him I was flying. (huh!)

3. If he asks you, (huh!) was I laughing, (huh!)
   If he asks you, (huh!) was I laughing, (huh!)
   If he asks you, (huh!) was I laughing, (huh!)
   Tell him I was crying, (huh!) tell him I was crying. (huh!)

4. Take this hammer, (huh!) and carry it to the captain, (huh!)
   Take this hammer, (huh!) and carry it to the captain, (huh!)
   Take this hammer, (huh!) and carry it to the captain, (huh!)
   Tell him I'm gone, (huh!) tell him I'm gone. (huh!)

The hammer songs created by the Negroes of the Southern states are among the finest work songs we know. They were work songs in every sense: they were sung at work; they described the work; they helped to make back-breaking work bearable. When gangs of slaves were swinging their picks or their sledgehammers under the blazing sun, the rhythm of a song could keep them moving more effectively than the whip of the overseer. With the first words the men would all swing their picks up in the air, and then as a phrase ended they would strike in unison, letting out their breath in a violent grunt.

There are many hammer songs, but this simple pattern was one of the most popular. This particular version was made famous by the great Negro folksinger, Huddie Ledbetter, commonly known as Leadbelly.

JOHN HENRY

1. When John Henry was a little baby
   Sitting on his pappy's knee
   He grabbed a hammer and a little piece of steel,
   Said, "This hammer'll be the death of me, Lord, Lord,
   This hammer'll be the death of me."

2. Now the captain said to John Henry,
   "I'm gonna bring that steam drill around,
   I'm gonna take that steam drill out on the job,
   I'm gonna whop that steel on down, Lord, Lord,
   Gonna whop that steel on down."

3. John Henry told his captain,
   "A man ain't nothing but a man,
   But before I'll let that steam drill beat me down
   I'll die with my hammer in my hand, Lord, Lord,
   I'll die with my hammer in my hand."

4. John Henry said to his shaker,
   "Now shaker, why don't you sing?
   'Cause I'm throwing twelve pounds from my hips on down,
   Just listen to that cold steel ring, Lord, Lord,
   Just listen to that cold steel ring."

5. The man that invented the steam drill,
   He thought he was mighty fine,
   But John Henry he made fourteen feet
   While the steam drill only made nine, Lord, Lord,
   The steam drill only made nine.

6. John Henry hammered on the mountain
   Till his hammer was striking fire.
   He drove so hard he broke his poor heart,
   Then he laid down his hammer and he died, Lord, Lord,
   He laid down his hammer and he died.

7. They took John Henry to the graveyard,
   And they buried him in the sand,
   And every locomotive comes rolling by
   Says, "There lies a steel-driving man,
     Lord, Lord
   There lies a steel-driving man."

8. Now some say he was born in Texas,
   And some say he was born in Maine,
   But I don't give a damn where that poor
     boy was born.
   He was a steel-driving man, Lord, Lord,
   He was a steel-driving man.

The greatest of the native North American ballads records the exploits of John Henry — that mighty steel-driving man. Most of the famous ballads of other lands celebrate noble lords and ladies, but in the New World the ballad-makers chose their greatest hero from the ranks of labor. Certainly no other song captures more vividly the indomitable spirit of the ordinary man.

The story of John Henry originated in West Virginia around 1872 when steel drivers were drilling the Big Bend Tunnel on the Chesapeake and Ohio Railroad. (In his book, *John Henry*, Guy Johnson explains: "A steel driver is a man who strikes a steel drill with a heavy hammer so as to sink the drill into rock or some other hard substance, thus making a hole into which an explosive can be inserted. A companion worker holds the drill in place and gives it occasional turns to make the cutting edge effective. This man is known as the turner or shaker.") Many people claimed to have known John Henry, but their accounts cannot be made to agree. Some say he was black, some say white. Some say he was of average size, others that he was a giant. They insist that he outdrove a steam-drill with his hammer and steel and died from the effort, although the real-life John Henry appears to have died in a cave-in.

As the legend spread, John Henry took on the characteristics of other folk heroes: on the Mississippi he was the strongest of the roustabouts; in the lumber camps he rivalled Paul Bunyan. Roark Bradford has written a colorful book describing his many adventures, and several researchers have sought to determine whether he was fact or fiction. The most thorough analysis is that of Louis Chappell: *John Henry, A Folklore Study* (1933). But the greatest memorial to him is the ballad which recounts his story in many and varying forms.

Whatever the details of his legend, John Henry has come to epitomize the millions of nameless workers who tamed the wilderness and built the world's mightiest industrial civilization on this new continent. He also symbolizes man's constant fear that he will be destroyed by the machines he has created. His battle to prevent the steam drill taking over the work of the steel drivers recalls the whole history of opposition to each new invention. In the nineteenth century, English hand-weavers, known as the Luddites, smashed the first automatic looms; today labor is increasingly concerned about the accelerating process of automation.

PAT WORKS ON THE RAILWAY

1. In eighteen hundred and forty-one
   I put my corduroy breeches on.
   I put my corduroy breeches on
   To work upon the railway.

   CHORUS: Fil-lee-me-oo-ree-i-ree-ay,
   Fil-lee-me-oo-ree-i-ree-ay,
   Fil-lee-me-oo-ree-i-ree-ay,
   To work upon the railway.

2. In eighteen hundred and forty-two
   I left the old world for the new.
   Bad 'cess to the luck that brought me through
   To work upon the railway.

3. In eighteen hundred and forty-three
   'Twas then I met sweet Biddy Magee.
   An elegant wife she's been to me
   While working on the railway.

4. In eighteen hundred and forty-four
   I landed on Columbia's shore,
   I landed on Columbia's shore
   To work upon the railway.

5. In eighteen hundred and forty-five
   I found myself more dead than alive.
   I found myself more dead than alive
   From working on the railway.

6. In eighteen hundred and forty-six
   I changed my trade to carrying bricks,
   I changed my trade to carrying bricks
   From working on the railway.

7. In eighteen hundred and forty-seven
   Sweet Biddy Magee she went to heaven.
   If she left one child she left eleven
   To work upon the railway.

In the 1830's and 1840's, when the first railroads were being built in the eastern United States, most of the work was done by Irishmen. That was the time when the great potato famines in Ireland drove thousands from their stricken country to seek their fortunes in America. Here they were put to work with pick and shovel, building the roadbeds for the many little stub lines that were later to be connected into trunk lines. So many Irishmen were hauling dirt and gravel that Emerson wrote then: "The poor Irishman — a wheelbarrow is his country."

This song has appeared in several versions, some of which were popular on the music-hall stage. It took to the sea where it became a capstan shanty, and it also became popular in England, for most of the British railways were also laid by Irish laborers. A recent questionnaire circulated in a number of locomotive sheds in northern England produced five versions of the song.

DRILL, YE TARRIERS, DRILL

Words and music by THOMAS F. CASEY

su - gar in your tay down be - hind the rail - way, And

drill, ye tar - ri - ers, drill! and blast! and fire!

2. The boss was a fine man down to the ground
   And he married a lady six feet 'round;
   She baked good bread, and she baked it well,
   But she baked it hard as the holes of hell!

3. Now the new foreman was Jean McCann;
   By God, he was a blamed mean man!
   Last week a premature blast went off,
   And a mile in the air went big Jim Goff.

4. The next time pay day came around,
   Jim Goff a dollar short was found.
   When he asked what for, came this reply:
   "You were docked for the time you were up in the sky."

John Henry fought the steam drill that threatened to throw thousands of Negroes out of their jobs, but the railroad workers who came after him learned how to use it. In the 1880's, the Irish tarriers, or dynamiters, were blasting their way through other mountains as the railways spread their gleaming lines across the continent.

While it is now considered an American folk song, "Drill Ye Tarriers, Drill" was apparently written by Thomas F. Casey, a New York entertainer who had himself worked on a blasting gang. It was first printed in 1888 and soon passed into oral tradition. It has turned up in many parts of the continent in localized versions, some of which change the refrain to "Drill Ye Heroes, Drill!"

The incident of the worker who was "docked for the time he was up in the sky" may be slightly exaggerated — but it symbolizes the conditions that existed in many industries before the workers organized themselves into unions.

JERRY, GO AND OIL THAT CAR

1. Come all ye railroad section men
   And listen to my song,
   It is of Larry O'Sullivan
   Who now is dead and gone.
   For twenty years a section boss,
   He never hired a tar.
   'Twas "joint ahead" and "center back,"
   And "Jerry, go and oil that car."

2. For twenty years a section boss,
   He worked upon the track,
   And be it to his credit,
   He never had a wreck,
   For he kept every joint right up to the point
   With a tap of the tamping bar,
   And while the b'ys were shimming up the ties,
   'Twas "Jerry, would you oil that car?"

3. And every Sunday morning
   Unto the gang he'd say,
   "Me b'ys, prepare ye, be aware,
   The old lady goes to church today.
   Now I want ev'ry man to pump the best he can,
   For the distance it is far,
   And we have to get in ahead of Number 10,
   So Jerry, go and oil that car."

4. 'Twas in November in the winter time,
   And the ground all covered with snow,
   He'd put the hand car on the track
   And over the section go.
   With his big soldier coat buttoned up to his throat
   All weathers he would dare,
   And 'twas "Paddy Mack, would you walk the track?"
   And "Jerry, go and oil that car."

5. God rest ye, Larry O'Sullivan,
   To me ye were kind and good.
   Ye always made the section men
   Go out and chop me wood,
   And fetch me water from the well
   And chop me kindling fine,
   And any man that wouldn't lend a hand,
   'Twas Larry'd give him his time.

6. "Give my respects to the Roadmaster,"
   Poor Larry he did cry,
   "And raise me up that I may see
   The old hand-car before I die.
   Then lay the spike maul on me chest,
   The gage and the old claw bar,
   And while the b'ys do be filling up the grave,
   Oh, Jerry, would you oil that car?"

The job of the section men is to keep the railroad track in good running order. Larry O'Sullivan obviously was a first-class section boss since he had no wreck in his twenty years. This old round-house song, which supposedly expressed the sentiments of Larry's widow, gives a good picture of the care required to keep the trains running safely. It was originally sung in an exaggerated Irish dialect which has been somewhat modified here.

When Carl Sandburg included the song in his *American Songbag* he noted: "In 1884 Charles Lummis heard Gunnysack Riley sing this at Albuquerque, New Mexico. Later, as an editor, he wanted the verses and put the matter up to Santa Fe railroad officials, who sent out a general order covering the whole system, calling for verses to 'Jerry Go An' Ile That Car.' A lost song was dug up . . ."

U. A. W.- C. I. O.

Words and music by
BESS AND BALDWIN HAWES

I was stan-ding round a de-fense town one day When I
thought I o-ver-heard a sol-dier say: "E-v'ry tank in our camp has that
U-A-dou-ble-U stamp, And I'm U-A-dou-ble-U too, I'm proud to say." It's the
U-A dou-ble U-C-I-O, makes the ar-my roll and go;

C7   F   C7   F

Tur - ning out the jeeps and tanks and air - planes e - v'ry day. It's the

F7   Bb   C7   F

U - A - dou-ble U - C - I - O, makes the ar - my roll and go, Puts wheels on the U. S. A.

2. I was there when the union came to town;
   I was there when old Henry Ford went down;
   I was standing by Gate Four when I heard the people roar,
   "They ain't gonna kick the autoworkers around."

3. I was there on that cold December day
   When we heard about Pearl Harbor far away;
   I was down in Cadillac Square when the union rallied there
   To put those plans for pleasure cars away.

4. There'll be a union label in Berlin
   When those union boys in uniform march in;
   And rolling in the ranks there'll be UAW tanks:
   Roll Hitler out and roll the union in.

The United Automobile Workers, now part of the AFL–CIO, is one of the largest unions in the world, with more than a million members. Author John Gunther has called it "the most volcanic union in the country." It has established large and powerful organizations in the automobile, air-craft, agricultural implement, and allied industries in both the United States and Canada, and has led the way for many unions in such collective bargaining fields as pensions, guaranteed annual wages, and regular productivity increases. It has also done exciting work in the fields of union education and political action, and has made dramatic use of radio and television.

Many songs have been written about the UAW and its turbulent history, beginning with the sit-down strikers of the 'thirties. One of the best describes the union's role during World War II when UAW members (aided of course by workers in steel, rubber, glass, electrical, and a dozen other industries) turned out an unbelievable mountain of planes, jeeps, and tanks to crush Hitler and his allies. This was another product of the Almanac Singers — only by that time most of the original members had dropped out and a new group had taken over. It included John Lomax's daughter Bess and her husband, Baldwin Hawes.

UNITED STEELWORKERS ARE WE

Words by M. T. MONTGOMERY

1. Oh, we are the men of the Steelworkers' Union,
   From blast furnace, open hearth, foundry, and mill,
   From ingot mould stripping, from scarfing and chipping,
   From out where the slag pots are dumped on the fill.

2. There's men from Cape Breton and men from Vancouver,
   Algoma and Stelco and old Montreal;
   There's men from Bell Island, from prairie and highland;
   United Steelworkers are we, one and all.

3. Now we dig the ore out and we run the smelter,
   We make the aluminum, pig iron, and steel,
   And we run the rail mills, the wire and nail mills—
   In industry Steelworkers are the "big wheel"!

4. We meet and we battle the toughest employers,
   At threats and injunctions and stooges we laugh;
   Our leaders are strongest, our locals fight longest;
   We have the best members, we have the best staff.

5. If you fancy licking the boots of the bosses,
   And for any favor their bidding you'll do;
   If you're just a piker and never a striker,
   The Steelworkers' Union is no place for you!

M. T. (Monty) Montgomery, education representative of the United Steelworkers in Canada, wrote this song after a weekend labor school on Bell Island, three miles off the coast of Newfoundland's Avalon Peninsula. He says: "Our members on Bell Island work in the Wabana Iron Mine. The 'Islanders' are great group singers and we sang for hour after hour each night. One favorite was 'The Squidjiggin' Ground' by Arthur Scammell, which is popular throughout Newfoundland. We must have sung it a hundred different times. When I returned to Toronto, the tune of 'The Squidjiggin' Ground' was still ringing in my ears, and I wrote this steelworkers' song to it." In Canada these verses are still sung to the tune of "The Squidjiggin' Ground," but because of copyright difficulties they are set here to a traditional Irish tune which is very similar to the Newfoundland song.

The United Steelworkers of America, with approximately one million members, is one of the great modern industrial unions which have developed in the last quarter century. The steelworkers' union includes iron-ore miners, men who turn this ore into ingots and sheet and rolled steel in the basic steel mills, and men who fabricate this steel into ten thousand items from paper clips to railroad cars.

MEN OF THE SOIL

Words by HAROLD HILDRETH,
HAROLD HATCHER and GERALD PATTON

Triumphantly
no chords

Men of the soil! We have la - bored un - end - ing, We have fed the world u - pon the

grain that we have grown. Now with the star of the new day as - cend - ing,

Gi - ants of the earth, at last we rise to claim our own. Jus - tice thru-out the land,

Hap - pi - ness as God has planned. Who is there de - nies our right to

reap where we have sown? Who is there de-nies our right to reap where we have sown?

2. Men of the soil! Now the torch we have lighted
   Kindles fire in every land where rings the harvest song!
   Shoulder to shoulder in courage united
   From every race we come to join the tillers' mighty throng.
       Earth ne'er shall eat again
       Bread gained through blood of men,
   We have sworn to right forevermore the ancient wrong.
   We have sworn to right forevermore the ancient wrong.

3. Men of the soil! We are coming in judgment
   To tell the world till justice rules there is no liberty!
   We in our strength are arising as prophets,
   Marching on to show the world the dawn that is to be.
       There's a lightning in the sky,
       There's a thunder shouting high;
   We will never stop until the sons of men are free.
   We will never stop until the sons of men are free.

"Men of the Soil" is one of the best-known farmers' songs, but few know where it came from. Chester Graham, Director of the Ashland Folk School at Grant, Michigan, from 1928-1938, gives the background.

The trail goes back to the summer of 1928 when a group attending the Ashland Folk School decided to translate "The Danish Harvest Song" (Marken er Mejet) into English. (The original can be heard on Folkway's record, "Songs of Denmark," FW 6857.) Carl Hutchison, a member of the group, took the song back to the Chicago Theological Seminary where he was teaching, and it became popular with the students there.

The following spring the farmers in the Chicago Milk Shed went on strike to force Chicago distributors to pay them the same price farmers were getting at Waukegan. A group of students from the Chicago Theological Seminary went out to help the farmers, and sang the Danish song at strike meetings. Then one night three of the students decided to write topical words to the Danish tune. The three were Gerald Patton (later in rural YMCA work in Michigan), Harold Hatcher (later secretary of the Illinois Farmers' Union), and Harold Hildreth (later on the Faculty of Syracuse University). They worked far into the night and then Patton and Hatcher went to bed, leaving Hildreth to complete the song. The result was "Men of the Soil," which is usually listed under Hildreth's name alone.

The song proved popular in the milk strike, was sung at Ashland Folk School in succeeding years, and soon became a special song of the Farmers' Union. Its stirring words and tune have won it wide recognition: in Canada it is used as the theme music of the CBC National Farm Broadcasts.

THE FARMER IS THE MAN

With a lilt

Oh, the far-mer comes to town with his wa-gon bro-ken down, but the far-mer is the man who feeds them all.—— If you'll on-ly look and see, I think you will ag-ree that the far-mer is the man who feeds them all. The far-mer is the man, the far-mer is the man, Lives on cre-dit till the

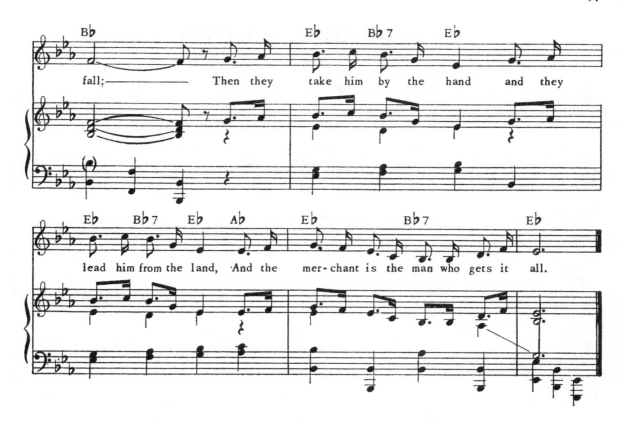

fall;— Then they take him by the hand and they

lead him from the land, And the mer-chant is the man who gets it all.

2. When the lawyer hangs around
   While the butcher cuts a pound,
   Oh, the farmer is the man who feeds them all,
   When the preacher and the cook
   Go a-strolling by the brook,
   Oh, the farmer is the man who feeds them all,

3. When the banker says he's broke
   And the merchant's up in smoke,
   They forget that it's the farmer
   feeds them all.
   It would put them to the test
   If the farmer took a rest;
   Then they'd know that it's the
   farmer feeds them all.

LAST CHORUS:
   The farmer is the man,
   The farmer is the man,
   Lives on credit till the fall —
   With the interest rate so high
   It's a wonder he don't die,
   For the mortgage man's the one
   who get it all.

This song, which originated among western farmers after the Civil War, is associated with such rural movements as the Grangers, the Greenback Party, and the Populists.

The National Grange of the Patrons of Husbandry was founded in 1867 for social and educational purposes, but local granges soon became political forums where economic grievances were aired. After the Panic of 1873, western and southern farmers grew poorer while eastern industrialists grew richer. The farmers blamed currency regulations for their plight and organized the Greenback Party, so-called because it demanded inflated currency to wipe out farm debts incurred during the previous period of high prices.

The Greenbacks faded after the election of 1884, and in 1891 the Populist Party was formed, with a platform calling for government ownership of railways and free coinage of silver. The eloquence of William Jennings Bryan captured most Populist votes for the Democrats in the election of 1896, and thereafter, increased farm prosperity led to the party's disappearance. However, the song associated with this period of farm protest is still remembered in many rural regions.

THE BOLL WEEVIL

With sly humor

The boll wee-vil is a lit-tle black bug Come from Mex-i-co they
say; Come all the way to Tex-as Just a-look-in' for a place to
stay. Just a-look-in' for a home, Just a-look-in' for a home,
Just a-look-in' for a home, Just a-look-in' for a home.

CHORUS

1. The boll weevil is a little black bug
   Come from Mexico they say,
   Come all the way to Texas
   Just a-lookin' for a place to stay.

CHORUS: Just a-lookin' for a home,
          Just a-lookin' for a home,
          Just a-lookin' for a home,
          Just a-lookin' for a home.

2. The first time I seen the boll weevil,
   He was settin' on the square;
   The next time I seen the boll weevil,
   He had all his family there.

CHORUS: Just a-lookin' for a home (4 times).

3. The farmer took the boll weevil
   And buried him in hot sand;
   The boll weevil say to the farmer,
   "I'll stand it like a man."

CHORUS: This'll be my home (4 times).

4. Then the farmer took the boll weevil
   And left him on the ice;
   The boll weevil say to the farmer,
   "This is mighty cool and nice."

CHORUS: This'll be my home (4 times).

5. The farmer took the boll weevil
   And fed him on paris green;
   The boll weevil say to the farmer,
   "It's the best I ever seen."

CHORUS: This'll be my home (4 times).

6. The boll weevil say to the farmer
   "You better let me alone;
   I et up all your cotton
   And now I'll start on the corn."

CHORUS: I'll have a home (4 times).

7. The merchant got half the cotton,
   The boll weevil got the rest;
   Didn't leave the poor old farmer
   But one old cotton dress.

CHORUS: And it's full of holes (4 times).

8. The farmer say to the merchant,
   "I ain't made but one bale,
   But before I'll give you that one,
   I'll fight and go to jail."

CHORUS: I'll have a home (4 times).

9. If anyone should ask you
   Who was it made this song,
   Tell him 'twas a poor farmer
   With a pair of blue duckin's on.

CHORUS: Ain't got no home (4 times).

Around 1900 the boll weevil crossed the Rio Grande into Texas and moved relentlessly across the Southern states, destroying the cotton plants which provided the only cash crop on most Southern farms.

Although it has caused more than a billion dollars worth of damage, the little black bug apparently inspires a reluctant admiration in his victims by his superhuman powers of resistance. Perhaps some Negro farmer was inspired to write this song because he saw in the boll weevil a prototype of his own struggle for survival. Whatever the reason, "The Ballad of the Boll Weevil" is so popular that it has been termed "the theme song of the Southern sharecropper."

Of it Carl Sandburg wrote:

"It never loses its strange overtones, with its smiling commentary on the bug that baffles the wit of man, with its whimsical point that while the boll weevil can make its home anywhere, the Negro, son of man, hath not where to lay his head . . . It is a paradoxical blend of moods: quickstep and dirge, hilarious defiance, and bowed resignation."

DOWN ON PENNY'S FARM

1. Come you ladies and you gentlemen and listen to my song;
   I'll sing it to you right but you might think it's wrong;
   May make you mad, but I mean no harm:
   It's all about the renters on Penny's farm.

CHORUS: It's hard times in the country,
   Down on Penny's farm.

2. Now you move out on Penny's farm,
   Plant a little crop of 'bacco and a little crop of corn.
   He'll come around to plan and plot
   Till he gets himself a mortgage on everything you got.

3. You go to the fields and you work all day,
   Till way after dark, but you get no pay.
   Promise you meat or a little lard,
   It's hard to be a renter on Penny's farm.

4. Now here's George Penny come into town
   With a wagon-load of peaches, not one of them sound.
   He's got to have his money or somebody's check;
   You pay him for a bushel and you don't get a peck.

5. Then George Penny's renters they come into town,
   With their hands in their pockets and their heads hanging down.
   Go in the store and the merchant will say:
   "Your mortgage is due and I'm looking for my pay."

6. Goes down in his pocket with a trembling hand —
   "Can't pay you all but I'll pay you what I can."
   Then to the telephone the merchant makes a call:
   "They'll put you on the chain gang if you don't pay it all."

The years after the Civil War saw the collapse of many great Southern plantations which had been built with slave labor. When the hard-pressed owners were forced to sell their land, much of it fell into the hands of hard businessmen who proceeded to break it up into small plots and rent these to "poor whites" or freed slaves. Sometimes those who actually farmed the land paid a yearly rental; others were under contract to give the landowner a certain share of their crops. But tenants and sharecroppers alike had a tough row to hoe. Their plots were too small to farm profitably, and once the landlord got his share they were left with too little to live on.

For many years the plight of the tenant farmers and sharecroppers was desperate enough to crush all hope, but they still had enough spirit to sing songs about it, and make bitter jokes like the sharecropper's invitation: "Come over to my house for dinner. We got a thousand things to eat, and every one of them's whippoorwill peas."

"Down on Penny's Farm" apparently owes something to the widespread lament known as "Hard Times in Cryderville Jail," but the parallel isn't as close as in "Hard Times in the Mill" (see Page 68). Alan Lomax found it as "Hard Times in the Country" on an old phonograph record made by the Bentley Boys in 1929. They are good examples of the many folk artists who appeared on commercial hillbilly and "race" records in the decade 1923-1933, before the Library of Congress began to collect field recordings for its Archive of American Folk Song.

John Greenway quotes very similar verses under the title, "Down on Robert's Farm," and says that Bascom Lunsford learned them "from Claude Reeves of Little River, Transylvania County, North Carolina, who wrote the song from personal experience, c. 1935."

PLANTING RICE

With choppy rhythm

Plant-ing rice is ne-ver fun, bent from morn till set of sun; Can-not
back is like to break, oh, my bones with damp-ness ache, And my

stand and can-not sit, can-not rest a lit-tle bit. Oh, my
legs are numb and set from the soak-ing in the

wet. Plant-ing rice is no fun, bent from morn till set of

sun. Can-not stand, can-not sit, can-not rest a lit-tle

bit. Oh, my back likes to break, oh, my bones with damp - ness

ache And my legs numb and set from the soak - ing in the wet.

1. Planting rice is never fun,
   Bent from morn till set of sun;
   Cannot stand and cannot sit,
   Cannot rest a little bit.
   Oh, my back is like to break,
   Oh, my bones with dampness ache,
   And my legs are numb and set
   From the soaking in the wet.

2. When the sun begins to break
   You will wonder as you wake
   In what muddy neighborhood
   There is work and pleasant food.
   It is hard to be so poor
   And such sore and pain endure.
   You must move your arms about
   Or you'll find you'll be without.

CHORUS: Planting rice is no fun,
Bent from morn till set of sun.
Cannot stand, cannot sit,
Cannot rest a little bit.
Oh, my back likes to break,
Oh, my bones with dampness ache,
And my legs numb and set
From the soaking in the wet.

Rice is the staff of life in the Far East, and planting rice is tough, back-breaking work. The planters have to stand in water and bend constantly as they move slowly along the rows.

In the Philippines they chant this song as they work in the rice fields. The music helps them to keep planting with a regular rhythm and breaks the monotony of the long day's work. It is customary for rice field owners to hire musicians to play and sing as the workers plant.

Joe Glazer learned this song from Cipriano Malanzo, President of the Philippine Trade Union Council.

ELEVEN CENT COTTON

Words and music by
BOB MILLER and EMMA DERMER

Pathetically

'Le-ven-cent cot-ton, for-ty cent meat, how in the world can a poor man eat?

Pray for the sun-shine, 'cause it will rain, things get-tin' worse, driv-in' us in-sane;

Built a nice house, paint-ed it brown; light-nin' came a-long and burnt it down.

No use talk-in', a-ny man's beat, with 'le-ven cent cot-ton and for-ty cent meat.

1. 'Leven-cent cotton, forty-cent meat,
How in the world can a poor man eat?
Pray for the sunshine, 'cause it will rain,
Things gettin' worse, drivin' us insane;
Built a nice house, painted it brown;
Lighnin' came along and burnt it down.
No use talkin', any man's beat
With 'leven-cent cotton and forty-cent meat.

2. 'Leven-cent cotton, forty-cent meat,
Keep gettin' thinner 'cause we don't eat;
Tried to raise peas, tried to raise beans;
All we can raise is turnip greens.
No corn in the crib, no chicks in the yard,
No meat in the smoke house, no tubs full of lard;
No use talkin', any man's beat
With 'leven-cent cotton and forty-cent meat.

3. 'Leven-cent cotton, forty-cent meat,
How in the world can a poor man eat?
Our clothes worn out, shoes run down,
Old slouch hat with a hole in the crown.
Poor gettin' poorer all around here,
Kids comin' regular ev'ry year;
No use talkin', any man's beat
With 'leven-cent cotton and forty-cent meat.

4. 'Leven-cent cotton, forty-cent meat,
How in the world can a poor man eat?
Mule's in the barn, no crop's laid by,
Corn crib empty and the cow's gone dry.
Well water's low, nearly out of sight,
Can't take a bath on a Saturday night.
No use talkin', any man's beat
With 'leven-cent cotton and forty-cent meat.

The farmer who raises a single cash crop — cotton, for example — is at the mercy of outside forces beyond his control which can bankrupt him in one season. Freak weather may lay waste his fields, or the plants may be attacked by the boll weevil or some equally destructive pest. And if he survives the weather and the bugs, prices may drop so low that he is plunged into debt.

Many generations of farmers have complained that the prices they get for their crops are far below the prices they have to pay — a complaint that in modern times has given rise to price subsidies and parity programs. But these devices were unknown when the poor farmer in the song had to sell his cotton for eleven cents a pound and pay forty cents for a pound of meat.

"Eleven-Cent Cotton" was written in 1928 by Bob Miller and Emma Dermer. This is a condensed version of their original song which circulated in many slightly varying forms during the depression. Then in 1940 it was parodied by the Almanac Singers as "Fifty Cent Butter and Fifty Cent Meat," with the prices being revised upwards as inflation continued.

ZUM GALI GALI

UNISON CHANT: Zum gali gali gali,
Zum gali gali,
Zum gali gali gali,
Zum gali gali.

Solo: 1. He-cha-lutz le'man a-vo-dah;
A-vo-dah le'man he-cha-lutz.

2. A-vo-dah le'man he-cha-lutz;
He-cha-lutz le'man a-vo-dah.

3. He-chalutz le'man ha-b'tulah;
Ha-b'tulah le'man he-cha-lutz.

This is one of the many work songs that have sprung up in the new nation of Israel where pioneer conditions have stimulated the people to sing of the joy of labor. In Europe for centuries restrictive laws prevented the Jews from becoming farmers; now in their ancient homeland they are reclaiming the desert wastes with determination and enthusiasm.

The words mean something like this: "The pioneer is for his work; work is for the pioneer. The pioneer is for his girl; his girl is for the pioneer."

SO LONG, IT'S BEEN GOOD TO KNOW YOU

Words and music by WOODY GUTHRIE

I've sung this song but I'll sing it a-gain Of the place that I lived on the wild win-dy plain, In the month called Ap-ril the coun-ty called Gray. Here's what all of the peo-ple there say: ———

CHORUS

So ——— long, it's been good to know you, So ——— long, it's

(over)

1. I've sung this song but I'll sing it again
   Of the place that I lived on the wild windy plain,
   In the month called April, the county called Gray,
   Here is what all of the people there say:

CHORUS: So long, it's been good to know you,
   So long, it's been good to know you,
   So long, it's been good to know you —
   This dusty old dust is a-getting my home
   And I've got to be drifting along.

2. A dust storm hit and it hit like thunder.
    It dusted us over and it covered us under,
    It blocked out the traffic, it blocked out the sun
    And straight for home all the people did run. (Singing:)

3. The sweethearts sat in the dark and sparked.
    They hugged and kissed in that dusty old dark.
    They sighed and cried, and hugged and kissed;
    Instead of marriage they talked like this:

4. The telephone rang and it jumped off the wall,
    And that was the preacher a-making his call.
    He said, "Kind friend, this might be the end;
    You've got your last chance at salvation from sin."

5. The church it was jammed, the church it was packed.
    That dusty old dust storm blowed so black
    That the preacher could not read a word of his text,
    So he folded his specs and took the collection. (Singing:)

This is the most famous of all Woody Guthrie's "dust-bowl ballads." His own comment about it was: "This actually happened in Pampa, Gray County, Texas, April 14, 1935. I was there. The storm was as black as tar and as big as an ocean. It looked like we was done for. Thousands of us packed up and lit out for safer territory."

Woody recorded the song in the late 'thirties in his Victor albums of "Dust Bowl Ballads" which soon became collectors' items. Then in 1951, "So Long, It's Been Good to Know You" landed on the Hit Parade when the Weavers recorded it for Decca in a slightly revised version.

ONE HAPPY SWEDE

Words by DONNA SHWARZROCK

1. Aye ban a farmer in Minnesota,
   Ban here mostly all my life,
   Got myself some fine contraptions
   Mostly to please my purty wife.

2. The REA she's sure ban helpful,
   Made our job here one big fun.
   All we do is press the buttons,
   Then our work by gosh she's done.

3. Got some milkers, sure are tricky,
   To my cows I put them on.
   Turn around and pet the calves,
   And then, by gol, my milkin's done.

4. Does my missus carry corn cobs,
   Chop her wood and get all in?
   I should say not, and why should she
   With her 'lectric stove, by gin.

5. Now that woman doesn't nag me
   For the water to go and get.
   All she does is turn the faucet
   And the whole durned place gets wet.

6. When she turns the 'lectric bulbs on
   For the neighbors all to see,
   Then I tell you this old farmstead
   Shines just like a Christmas tree.

7. All I need to make me happy
   Is that thing they call TV;
   With the money "our line" saves me
   I can get one soon, by gee.

8. Now this REA is something;
   With it you just can't go wrong,
   But I tell you, and I mean it,
   This ole Swede helped things along.

In 1935, only 15 per cent of the farms in the United States had electricity. By 1957, the number had reached 95 per cent. The force behind this farm revolution was REA — Rural Electrification Administration — established by the federal government in 1935 to bring low-cost power to rural areas long ignored by private power companies who preferred to concentrate on the more profitable urban areas.

More than a thousand successful electrical co-ops have been established as a result of the long-term low-interest loans made available by REA, and today electricity has eliminated much of the drudgery and back-breaking work that were part of the farm family's life.

For the farmer, REA meant power to run the water pumps, the food choppers, the electric brooders, and the milking machines. For his wife, it meant electric stoves, washing machines, refrigerators, and sewing machines, not to mention irons, toasters, and percolators. And of course it also brought electric lights, electric furnaces, radio, and television.

Donna Schwarzrock, a farm housewife of Hector, Minnesota, wrote "One Happy Swede" in 1953 for a song-writing contest conducted by the National Rural Electric Cooperative Association (NRECA) — the central body of REA co-ops. Sung to the tune of "Reuben and Rachel," it is featured in the NRECA "Song Book."

BLOW YE WINDS IN THE MORNING

Vigorously

'Tis ad-ver-tised in Bos-ton, New York, and Buf-fa-lo, Five

hun-dred brave A-me-ri-cans a-whal-ing for to go. Sing-ing

CHORUS

Blow ye winds, in the mor-ning, Blow ye winds, high-o!

Clear a-way your run-ning gear And blow, boys, blow!

1. 'Tis advertised in Boston, New York, and Buffalo,
   Five hundred brave Americans a-whaling for to go.

CHORUS: Singing blow ye winds in the morning,
         Blow ye winds, high-o!
         Clear away your running gear
         And blow, boys, blow!

2. They send you to New Bedford, that famous whaling port,
   And give you to some land-sharks to board and fit you out.

3. They tell you of the clipper-ships a-going in and out,
   And say you'll take five hundred sperm before you're six months out.

4. It's now we're out to sea, my boys, the wind comes on to blow;
   One half the watch is sick on deck, the other half below.

5. But as for the provisions, we don't get half enough;
   A little piece of stinking beef and a blamed small bag of duff.

6. Next comes the running rigging, which you're all supposed to know;
   'Tis "Lay aloft, you son-of-a-gun, or overboard you go!"

7. The skipper's on the quarter-deck a-squinting at the sails
   When up aloft the lookout sights a school of spouting whales.

8. "Now clear away the boats, my boys, and after him we'll travel,
   But if you get too near his fluke, he'll kick you to the devil!"

9. Now we have got him turned up, we tow him alongside;
   We over with our blubber-hooks and rob him of his hide.

10. Next comes the stowing down, my boys; 'twill take both night and day,
    And you'll all have fifty cents apiece on the hundred and ninetieth lay.

11. When we get home, our ship made fast, and we get through our sailing,
    A winding glass around we'll pass and damn this blubber whaling!

Whaling was one of the first great industries of North America, and for many years New Bedford, Massachusetts, was the world's leading whaling port. It was a hard and dangerous trade, for voyages often lasted two or three years and boats were often smashed to bits by the thrashing of the whale. The men were harshly treated and the food was poor — the "duff" mentioned (Verse 5) often consisted of hardtack pounded up with molasses in a bag. Instead of wages, the men received a share in the profits of the voyage — but after all expenses were deducted the profits were sometimes mighty slim. The shares were called "lays" and varied according to the man's position: that is, if the profits were divided into two hundred lays, the captain might get ten and the ordinary sailor one.

The description given here of the catching and killing of the whale is quite accurate. After he was harpooned by the sailors who went after him in the small whaleboat, he was hauled to the larger ship and hoisted alongside by a chain around his tail (or fluke). Then the "cutting in" and "stowing away" would begin. The head was cut apart and brought aboard: to get the valuable sperm oil, the men had to climb into the head and work waist-deep in the loose fat. The blubber was peeled from the carcass in huge strips weighing a ton or more, and then cut up into small pieces to be stowed in barrels or oil tanks. The decks would usually be awash with oil, and the stench was unbelievable. Work would continue without rest until the fifteen tons or more of oil were safely stowed below decks.

The tune for "Blow Ye Winds" was borrowed from an old English song that was a variant of "The Baffled Knight" (Child 56).

LEAVE HER, JOHNNY!

1. I thought I heard the Old Man say,
    Leave her, Johnny, leave her!
  You can go ashore and draw your pay,
    It's time for us to leave her.

2. The winds were foul, the work was hard,
    Leave her, Johnny, leave her!
  From Liverpool docks to the Brooklyn yard,
    It's time for us to leave her.

3. The winds were foul, the ship was slow,
    Leave her, Johnny, leave her!
  The grub was bad and the wages low,
    It's time for us to leave her.

4. She shipped it green and she made us curse—
    Leave her, Johnny, leave her!
  The mate is a devil and the old man worse,
    It's time for us to leave her.

5. The rats have gone, and we the crew,
    Leave her, Johnny, leave her!
  It's time, by God, that we went too,
    It's time for us to leave her.

Sea shanties form one of the largest group of work songs, and many of them describe the hardships aboard the wooden sailing vessels. "Leave Her, Johnny" was usually the most outspoken for it was the sailors' farewell song at the end of a voyage. After a sailing ship had reached port she had to be pumped dry before the crew went ashore, and this was the song always used to accompany that final task. As they were safe in dock, the men felt free to express their opinions of their officers and the treatment they had received.

LOW BRIDGE, EVERYBODY DOWN

(over)

Low bridge! E-v'ry-bo-dy down, Low bridge! we're com-ing to a town. You will al-ways know your neigh-bor; you'll al-ways know your pal If you've e-ver na-vi-ga-ted on the E-rie Ca-nal.—

1. I've got a mule and her name is Sal,
   Fifteen miles on the Erie Canal;
   She's a good old worker and a good old pal,
   Fifteen miles on the Erie Canal.
   We've hauled some barges in our day,
   Filled with lumber, coal, and hay,
   And we know every inch of the way
   From Albany to Buffalo.

CHORUS: Low bridge! Everybody down!
Low bridge! We're coming to a town.
You'll always know your neighbor; you'll always know your pal
If you've ever navigated on the Erie Canal.

2. We'd better get on our way, old pal,
   Fifteen miles on the Erie Canal.
   You can bet your life I'd never part with Sal,
   Fifteen miles on the Erie Canal.
   Get us there, Sal, here comes a lock;
   We'll make Rome 'fore six o'clock.
   One more trip and back we'll go,
   Right back home to Buffalo.

When the first settlers moved inland from the Atlantic Coast they followed the Hudson Valley to Albany and then spread across to the Great Lakes. In 1817, New York State undertook to build a canal linking Albany to the Great Lake Port of Buffalo, and the 340-mile ditch was opened in 1825. During the next twenty years the population of Michigan and Ohio soared and most of the new settlers and their goods moved west along the Erie Canal.

By 1845, 4,000 boats employing some 25,000 canalers were carrying not only "lumber, coal, and hay" but a thousand other commodities. The boats were pulled by mules or horses who plodded along the towpath at a speed of three to four miles an hour. The mule-driver had little to do but watch for low-bridges: according to Carl Carmer, "Riders on the slow canal boats got many a bruised cranium from failing to heed the warning cry of the 'hoggie' or mule-driver — 'Low bridge, everybody down!' "

The most popular song of the canalers was the satiric description of "the terrible storm we had one night on the E-ri-ee Canal," but this other canal song — a tribute to a faithful mule — gives a more accurate picture of the long monotonous hours of hauling.

Although it has long been considered a folk song, Dr. Harold W. Thompson, an expert on the folklore of New York State, says that "Low Bridge, Everybody Down" was published by Thomas S. Allen in 1913, when traffic on the Erie was already waning. Sandburg included it in his *American Songbag* with the comment that he had heard it sung "movingly, meditatively, so that the Erie Canal took on the character of a symbol of life as a highway to be taken ploddingly with steady pulse." Walter Edmonds also used the song in his novel, *Rome Haul* (1929), later made into a movie as "The Farmer Takes a Wife."

118

CANADAY-I-O

1. "Come all ye jolly fellows, how would you like to go
   And spend one winter in the woods of Canaday-I-O?"
   "We're going up to Canaday," is what we young men say,
   "And going up to Canaday depends upon the pay."

2. "It's sure we'll pay good wages; we'll pay your passage out,
   But you must sign the papers that you will stay the route,
   For if you should get homesick, and say back home you'll go,
   We will not pay your passage from Canaday-I-O."

3. We had a pleasant journey on the route we had to go
   And landed in Three Rivers in Canaday-I-O.
   Oh, then the Norcross agent, he came a-prowling round
   And said, "My jolly fellows, why don't you all lie down?"

4. Our hearts were made of iron; our souls were cased with steel;
   The hardships of that winter could never make us yield.
   Our food the dogs would bark at; our beds were on the snow —
   We suffered worse than poison in Canaday-I-O.

5. And now the winter's over, it's homeward we are bound,
   And in this cursed country we'll never more be found.
   Go back to your wives and sweethearts, tell others not to go
   To that God-forsaken country called Canaday-I-O.

This is one of the many lumberjack songs reflecting conditions in the lumber camps of Canada and the United States. It probably originated in the 1850's when shantyboys from Maine were recruited to work in winter camps along the St. Lawrence. It is thought to have been written by a Maine man called Ephraim Braley who went up to "Canaday-I-O" in 1853, and he patterned it on an old English sea song called "Canada-I-O" which, in its turn, was based on a still older love song called "Caledonia." Soon the lumberman's complaint spread to other camps, taking on new forms as it travelled. In Ontario and the states bordering on the Great Lakes it told of hardships suffered in "Michigan-I-O." Then it reached the plains and was transformed into "The Buffalo Skinners" (see next page). Railroad men also took it up and told of their troubles when they went to work on "The Oregon Short Line Way Out in Idaho," and the cowboys used it for a song about "The Hills of Mexico."

THE BUFFALO SKINNERS

Vigorously

'Twas in the town of Jacks-bo-ro in the spring of se-ven-ty-three, A man by the name of Cre-go came step-ping up to me, Say-ing, "How do you do, young fel-low, and how would you like to go And spend the sum-mer plea-sant-ly on the range of the buf-fa-lo?"

1. 'Twas in the town of Jacksboro in the spring of seventy-three,
   A man by the name of Crego came stepping up to me,
   Saying, "How do you do, young fellow, and how would you like to go
   And spend the summer pleasantly on the range of the buffalo?"

2. And me not having any job, to old Crego I did say,
   "This going out on the buffalo range depends upon the pay.
   But if you will pay good wages, give transportation too,
   I think that I will go with you to the range of the buffalo."

3. "Yes, I will pay good wages, give transportation too,
   Provided you will go with me and stay the summer through;
   But if you should grow homesick, come back to Jacksboro,
   I won't pay transportation from the range of the buffalo."

4. Our meat it was of buffalo hump, like iron was our bread,
   And all we had to sleep on was a buffalo for a bed;
   The fleas and gray-backs worked on us, and boys, they were not slow;
   I tell you there's no worse hell on earth than the range of the buffalo.

5. Our hearts were cased with buffalo hocks, our souls were cased with steel;
   The hardships of that summer would nearly make us reel.
   While skinning the damned old stinkers, our lives they had no show
   For the Indians waited to pick us off on the hills of Mexico.

6. The season being over, old Crego he did say
   The crowd had been extravagant, was in debt to him that day.
   We coaxed him and we begged him and still it was no go —
   We left old Crego's bones to bleach on the range of the buffalo.

7. It's now we've crossed Pease River and homeward we are bound.
   No more in that hell-fired country shall ever we be found
   Go home to our wives and sweethearts, tell others not to go.
   For God's forsaken the buffalo range and the damned old buffalo.

When the white men reached the great plains of North America, a new occupation came into being: that of buffalo hunting. At that time the herds of buffalo were so large that they turned the prairie black as far as a man could see. Stimulated by a U. S. government bounty on buffalo hides, parties of hunters swarmed over the plains, killing the sluggish animals by the thousands. They skinned the carcasses and shipped the hides east to be made into rugs and coats, leaving the bones to bleach on the prairies.

From the adventures of one party of buffalo skinners came what Professor George Kittredge has called "the greatest of the Western ballads." The tune and the pattern were borrowed from the lumbering song known as "Canaday-I-O" or "Michigan-I-O," but the words have taken on a more epic quality.

Cowboys shunned the Texas City of Jacksboro which was the buffalo skinners' hangout, saying, "If them buffalo hunters don't kill ye for money, they'll kill ye for meanness." John Lomax, who collected this song, quotes a former buffalo hunter who claimed to have been on the expedition in question:

"It was a hell of a trip down Pease River, lasting several months. We fought sand-storms, flies, bed-bugs, wolves, and Indians. At the end of the season old Crego announced he had lost money and could not pay us off. We argued the question with him. He didn't see our side of things, so we shot him down and left his damned old bones to bleach where we had left so many stinking buffalo. On the way back to Jacksboro, one of the boys started up a song about the trip and the hard times and old Crego, and we all set in to help him. Before we got back to Jacksboro we had shaped it up and the whole crowd could sing it."

The song's vivid picture of labor conditions in an early American industry merits a place here. Then, as now, we find the workers having trouble with the boss, but the method they used to settle their wage dispute would not be generally acceptable today.

THE OLD CHISHOLM TRAIL

1. Come along boys, and listen to my tale,
   And I'll tell you of my troubles on the old Chisholm Trail

CHORUS: Come a ti yi yippy yippy yi yippi yea,
   Come a ti yi yippy yippy yea.

2. With a ten-dollar horse and a forty-dollar saddle
   I'm going down to Texas for to punch them cattle.

3. I woke up one morning on the old Chisholm Trail,
   A rope in my hand and a cow by the tail.

4. I started up the trail October twenty-third,
   I started up the trail with the 2-U herd.

5. I'm in my saddle before daylight
   And before I sleep the moon shines bright.

6. It's cloudy in the west, a-looking like rain,
   And my damned old slicker's in the wagon again.

7. The wind began to blow, the rain began to fall,
   It looked, by grab, like we was going to lose them all.

8. I jumped in the saddle and grabbed hold the horn,
   Best damned cow-puncher ever was born.

9. Oh, it's bacon and beans most every day —
   I'd as soon be eating prairie hay.

10. There's a stray in the herd and the boss said kill it,
    So I shot him in the rump with the handle of a skillet.

11. My feet in the stirrup and my hand on the horn,
    I'm the best damned cowboy ever was born.

12. I went to the boss to draw my roll,
    He figgered me out nine dollars in the hole.

13. A-roping and a-tying and a-branding all day,
    I'm working mighty hard for mighty little pay.

14. So I went to the boss and we had a little chat,
    And I hit him in the face with my big slouch hat.

15. So the boss says to me, "Why, I'll fire you,
    Not only you, but the whole damn crew."

16. So I rounded up the cowboys and we had a little meeting,
    We all took a vote and the boss took a beating.

17. So we organized a union and it's going mighty strong,
    The boss minds his business and we all get along.

18. With my knees in the saddle and my seat in the sky,
    I'll quit punching cows in the sweet by-and-by.

In the great age of cowpunching — from 1870 to 1890 — some twelve million longhorn cattle were driven up "the old Chisholm Trail." The trail began down at San Antonio and wound north through Texas to the railhead at Dodge City, Kansas, where some cattle were shipped east. Other herds were pushed on up to Cheyenne, Wyoming, and then the trail branched out to Montana, Idaho, and the Dakotas where the richer grass provided good pasture to fatten the cattle before they were sold.

There were often two or three thousand cattle in a herd, and the trip up the trail might last for five months. As the cowboys rode along in the choking prairie dust behind an endless stream of cows, the only way they could relieve their boredom was by singing. Their favorite song was "The Old Chisholm Trail" in which they could record every incident of the interminable trip. There are literally hundreds of different verses, many of them unprintable. "It's as long as the cattle trail from Texas to Wyoming," remarked one cowboy to John Lomax after he had sung sixty-nine verses without stopping.

The first fifteen verses have been chosen from the many traditional ones collected by the Lomaxes and others. Verses 16 and 17 originated with Tony Kraber who recorded them in his album of cowboy songs called "The Old Chisholm Trail."

HARD TRAVELING

Words and music by WOODY GUTHRIE

1. I been havin' some hard travelin', I thought you knowed;
   I been havin' some hard travelin', way down the road.
   I been havin' some hard travelin', hard ramblin', hard gamblin' —
   I been havin' some hard travelin', Lord

2. I been doin' some hard-rock minin', I thought you knowed;
   I been leanin' on a pressure drill, way down the road.
   Hammer flyin', air-hose suckin', six feet o' mud an' I sure been a-muckin'—
   I been havin' some hard travelin', Lord.

3. I been workin' that Pittsburgh steel, I thought you knowed;
   I been pourin' that red hot slag, way down the road.
   I been blastin', I been firin', I been duckin' red-hot iron —
   I been havin' some hard travelin', Lord.

4. I been riding' them fast rattlers, I thought you knowed;
   I been ridin' them flat wheelers, way down the road.
   I been ridin' them dead enders, blind passengers, pickin' up cinders —
   I been havin' some hard travelin', Lord.

5. I been layin' in a hard-rock jail, I thought you knowed;
   I been layin' out ninety days, way down the road.
   Mean old judge, he says to me: "Ninety days for vagrancy"—
   I been havin' some hard travelin', Lord.

6. I been hittin' some hard harvestin', I thought you knowed;
   North Dakota to Kansas City, way down the road.
   Cuttin' that wheat, stackin' that hay, tryin' to make 'bout a dollar a day —
   I been havin' some hard travelin', Lord.

7. I been hittin' that Lincoln Highway, I thought you knowed;
   I been hittin' that Sixty-Six, way down the road.
   Heavy load and a worried mind, lookin' for a woman that's hard to find —
   I been havin' some hard travelin', Lord.

Woody Guthrie has written more than a thousand songs, but none tells his story better than this one. Says Woody:

> " 'Hard Traveling' is the kind of a song you would sing after you had been booted off your little place and had lost out, lost everything, hocked everything down at the pawnshop, and had bummed a lot of stems asking for work. . . . It is a song about the hard traveling of the working people, not the moonstruck traveling of the professional vacationers. It tells about a man who has ridden the flat wheels, kicked up cinders, dumped the red-hot slag, hit the hard-rock tunneling, the hard harvesting, the hard-rock jail."

Woody has had some hard traveling since he was born in Okemah, Oklahoma, in 1912. As a boy he sold newspapers, danced street jigs, and sang for pennies. He shined shoes and cleaned spittoons. He has traveled back and forth across the continent in old jalopies and freight cars. He has known first-hand the dust bowl, the displaced farmer, the migratory worker. He has been a laborer, a sailor, a wanderer. He saw poverty, misery, cruelty, and injustice, and he dedicated his poetic genius to telling the story of the "hard travelers" with his voice and his guitar. (For details about Woody's own "hard traveling," see his autobiography, *Bound for Glory*.)

The Library of Congress has described him as "our best contemporary ballad composer," and when Woody put out his first Asch record album in 1944, John Steinbeck wrote in the introduction:

> "Woody is just Woody. Thousands of people do not know he has any other name. He is just a voice and a guitar. He sings the songs of a people and I suspect that he is, in a way, that people. Harsh-voiced and nasal, his guitar banging like a tire iron on a rusty rim, there is nothing sweet about Woody, and there is nothing sweet about the songs he sings. But there is something more important for those who will listen. There is the will of a people to endure and fight against oppression."

HALLELUJAH, I'M A BUM

1. Oh, why don't you work, like other men do?
   How the hell can I work when there's no work to do?

CHORUS: Hallelujah, I'm a bum,
              Hallelujah, bum again!
              Hallelujah, give us a handout
              To revive us again!

2. I went to a house; I knocked on the door;
   The lady said, "Scram, bum, you've been here before!"

3. I went to a house; I asked for some bread;
   The lady came out, said, "The baker is dead."

4. Oh, I love my boss; he's a good friend of mine;
   That's why I am starving out on the bread line.

5. Oh, why don't you save all the money you earn?
   If I didn't eat, I'd have money to burn.

For half a century, "Hallelujah, I'm a Bum" has been popular among hoboes, Wobblies, and the general public. Its jocular, irreverent spirit is in sharp contrast to the original hymn from which the song derives:

    "Hallelujah, Thine the glory,
    Hallelujah, Amen,
    Hallelujah, Thine the glory,
    Revive us again!"

The English musical historian, Reginald Nettel, says that the tune is found in the overture to "The Miller and His Men," an English opera by Sir Henry Bishop dating from 1813.

For years "Hallelujah, I'm a Bum" was considered a folk song authored by no one in particular —at least no one whose identity was known. However, Harry McClintock, an old Wobbly songleader who recorded the song in 1926, has made a good case for his authorship.

While hoboing on the open road in 1897 or 1898, bumming his meals or singing for his supper, McClintock says he put new words to "Revive Us Again," and called it "Hallelulia on the Bum":

    "There were only two or three verses at first but new ones practically wrote themselves. The jungle stiffs liked the song and so did the saloon audiences, most of whom had hit the road at one time or another, and the rollicking, devil-may-care lilt of the thing appealed to them."

During the Spanish American War, McClintock says, he sang the song in an army training camp in Tennessee, and the soldiers took it up, adding new verses. After the war they helped to spread the song around the country. By the late 1920's, more than a dozen publishers had turned out sheet music of the song. McClintock then charged them with infringement of copyright, and managed to establish his authorship legally. (For a detailed account of McClintock's claim see Greenway's *American Folk Songs of Protest*, pp. 197-203.)

At the 1908 convention of the IWW, the Spokane radicals sang "Hallelujah I'm a Bum," and were promptly dubbed "the bummery" by Daniel DeLeon, leader of the Socialist Labor Party.

During the depression of the thirties when millions were unemployed and tens of thousands went "on the bum," this song could be heard from coast to coast.

GOING DOWN THE ROAD

1. I'm goin' down the road feelin' bad,
   I'm goin' down the road feelin' bad,
   I'm goin' down the road feelin' bad, Lord, Lord,
   And I ain't gonna be treated this a-way.

2. I'm goin' where them dust storms never blow,
   I'm goin' where them dust storms never blow,
   I'm goin' where them dust storms never blow, Lord, Lord,
   And I ain't gonna be treated this a-way.

3. I'm goin' where the climate suits my clothes,
   I'm goin' where the climate suits my clothes,
   I'm goin' where the climate suits my clothes, Lord, Lord,
   And I ain't gonna be treated this a-way.

4. I'm a-lookin' for a job with honest pay,
   I'm a-lookin' for a job with honest pay,
   I'm a-lookin' for a job with honest pay, Lord, Lord,
   And I ain't gonna be treated this a-way.

5. These two-dollar shoes hurt my feet,
   These two-dollar shoes hurt my feet,
   These two-dollar shoes hurt my feet, Lord, Lord,
   And I ain't gonna be treated this a-way.

6. But ten-dollar shoes fit 'em neat,
   But ten-dollar shoes fit 'em neat,
   But ten-dollar shoes fit 'em neat, Lord, Lord,
   And I ain't gonna be treated this a-way.

7. I'm goin' where the water tastes like wine,
   I'm goin' where the water tastes like wine,
   I'm goin' where the water tastes like wine, Lord, Lord,
   And I ain't gonna be treated this a-way.

8. The water here, it tastes like turpentine,
   The water here, it tastes like turpentine,
   The water here, it tastes like turpentine, Lord, Lord,
   And I ain't gonna be treated this a-way.

9. I'm goin' down the road feelin' bad,
   I'm goin' down the road feelin' bad,
   I'm goin' down the road feelin' bad, Lord, Lord,
   And I ain't gonna be treated this a-way.

The first and hardest-hit victims of the Great Depression were the farmers in the dry western prairies. To the unemployed of the cities, that era was "the hungry 'thirties," but to western dirt farmers it was "the dirty 'thirties." Driven from their homes by dust storms and grasshoppers and mortgage companies, they loaded their few possessions into broken-down jalopies and headed down the road "looking for a job at honest pay." They were America's "displaced persons" long before the term "DP" became a familiar label in the Old World. They were the Joads, whose tragic history was immortalized by John Steinbeck in *Grapes of Wrath*. John Greenway reports:

> "While directing the filming of the *Grapes of Wrath*, John Ford needed background music for a group scene. He asked the Okies whom he had recruited as character extras to sing something that was known to every Okie, Arkie, and Mizoo. Without hesitation, they began singing 'Goin' Down the Road Feelin' Bad.'"

This old blues song had long been a favorite with America's tramps, hoboes, and Wobblies, but it took on a new lease of life because it so well described the plight of the dust-bowl refugees.

SOUP SONG

With humor

Words by JOE GLAZER

'Way back in the days of de - pres - sion,——— I did - n't have nu - thin' to eat,——— But that did - n't bo - ther me, Mis - ter,——— I was fed from my head to my feet ——— with

CHORUS

Soo - oop, soo - oop, They gave me a

bowl of soo - oop; Soo - oop,,

soo - oop, They gave me a bowl of soup. ————

2. One day the depression was over,
   I almost was back on my feet,
   But quickly there came a recession,
   So once more I started to eat—

3. We're striking this mill for a living,
   And one thing on which you can bet
   Is that if we don't stick together
   There's only one thing we will get—

FINAL CHORUS: Soo-oop, soo-oop,
               They'll give you a bowl of soo-oop;
               So-oop, soo-oop,
               They'll give you a bowl of soup!

The soup line has long been a symbol of hard times. During the depression of 1914 Joe Hill wrote a popular soup-line song to the tune of "It's a Long, Long Way to Tipperary":

"It's a long way down to the soup line,
It's a long way to go.
It's a long, long way down to the soup line
And the soup is thin I know.

"Good-bye, good old pork chops,
Farewell, beefsteak rare;
It's a long, long way down to the soup line,
But my soup is there."

Another soup song to the tune of "My Bonnie Lies Over the Ocean" appeared during the great depression of the 'thirties. Then the plight of hundreds of thousands of unemployed men was described in verses like this:

"I'm spending my nights at the flophouse,
I'm spending my days on the street.
I'm looking for work, and I find none;
I wish I had something to eat."

In 1945, Joe Glazer rewrote the depression "Soup Song" in the form given here.

BEANS, BACON, AND GRAVY

With pathos

I was born long a-go in eigh-teen nine-ty-one, and I've seen ma-ny a pa-nic, I will own. I've been hun-gry I've been cold, and now I'm grow-ing old, But the worst I've seen is nine-teen thir-ty one. Oh, those

CHORUS

beans, ba-con, and gra-vy, they al-most drive me cra-zy! I

eat them till I see them in my dreams. When I wake up in the mor-ning and a-

no-ther day is daw-ning, Then I know I'll have a-no-ther mess of beans.

2. We all congregate each morning
   At the county barn at dawning,
   And everyone is happy, so it seems.
   But when our work is done
   We file in one by one
   And thank the Lord for one more mess of
      beans.

3. We have Hooverized on butter,
   And for milk we've only water,
   And I haven't seen a steak in many a day.
   As for pies, cakes, and jellies,
   We substitute sow-bellies
   For which we work the county road each
      day.

4. If there ever comes a time
   When I have more than a dime,
   They will have to put me under lock and key,
   For they've had me broke so long
   I can only sing this song
   Of the workers and their misery.

The records of most depressions are preserved in song — sad, bitter, or humorous. These songs often tell the story of unemployment and misery more effectively than a scholarly sociological survey.

Dozens of songs, perhaps hundreds, were made up during the Great Depression of 1929-1933. One of the better ones is "Beans, Bacon, and Gravy." The tune is similar to the melody of the folk ballad, "Jesse James."

During the depression many sharecroppers and unemployed would have considered a diet of "Beans, Bacon, and Gravy" quite luxurious. Lee Hays tells of a Negro in East Arkansas who made an impromptu speech at a union meeting: "I have worked fifty years and all I ever got to show for it is beans. Well, I'm glad I like beans, because I get beans. That's all I get. I'm bean rich. Work all year, make a crop, and at settling time what do I get? Dollars? Beans! All I want before I die is one little old piece of meat. To put in my beans."

FOUR PENCE A DAY

By permission of Ewan MacColl.

1. The ore is waiting in the tubs, the snow's upon the fell;
   Canny folks are sleeping yet, but lead is reet to sell.
   Come, my little washer lad, come let's away,
   We're bound down to slavery for fourpence a day.

2. It's early in the morning we rise at five o'clock,
   And the little slaves come to the door to knock, knock, knock.
   Come, my little washer lad, come let's away;
   It's very hard to work for fourpence a day.

3. My father was a miner and lived down in the town;
   'Twas hard work and poverty that always kept him down.
   He aimed for me to go to school, but brass he couldn't pay,
   So I had to go to the washing rake for fourpence a day.

4. Fourpence a day, my lad, and very hard to work,
   And never a pleasant look from a gruffy-looking Turk.
   His conscience it may fail and his heart it may give way,
   Then he'll raise us our wages to ninepence a day.

It is hard to realize today that less than a century ago small children worked twelve or fourteen hours in the mines. Little tots of four, five, and six worked as "trapper boys," sitting all day in the dark passages, ready to open and shut the trap-doors regulating the ventilation of the mine, to allow coal and colliers to pass through. Slightly older boys dragged tubs of coal along the ways or separated the slate from the coal.

On May 17, 1877, the *Labor Standard* described the breaker room in the Hickory Colliery, near St. Clair, Pennsylvania:

"In a little room in this big, black shed — a room not twenty feet square — forty boys are picking their lives away. The floor of the room is an inclined plane, and a stream of coal pours constantly in. They work here, in this little black hole, all day and every day, trying to keep cool in summer, trying to keep warm in winter, picking away among the black coals, bending over till their little spines are curved, never saying a word all the livelong day. These little fellows go to work in this cold dreary room at seven o'clock in the morning and work till it is too dark to see any longer. For this they get $1 to $3 a week. Not three boys in this roomful could read or write. Shut in from everything that is pleasant, with no chance to learn, with no knowledge of what is going on about them, with nothing to do but work, grinding their little lives away in this dusty room, they are no more than the wire screens that separate the great lumps of coal from the small. They have no games; when their day's work is done they are too tired for that. They know nothing but the difference between slate and coal."

Similarly, on the other side of the ocean, in the Yorkshire lead mines, the ore-bearing rocks were separated from the clay and gravel in washing rakes operated by young boys or old disabled miners, and, as this fine old British song tells us, they were paid the munificent wage of "Fourpence a Day." The song is attributed to Thomas Raine, lead-miner and bard of Teesdale, and it is said that the mine owners became so incensed by it that they closed the pits and imported lead-miners from Germany. The song probably dates back more than a hundred years. Ewan MacColl noted it from the singing of a retired lead-miner in Yorkshire.

LIFE IS A TOIL

With a lilt

One day as I wan-dered, I heard a com-plain-ing, and saw an old

wo-man, the pic-ture of gloom. She gazed at the mud on her

door-step ('twas rain-ing) and this was her song as she wiel-ded her broom:

CHORUS

"Oh, life is a toil and love is a trou-ble, And beau-ty will

2. "It's sweeping at six and it's dusting at seven;
   It's victuals at eight and it's dishes at nine.
   It's potting and panning from ten to eleven;
   We scarce break our fast till we plan how to dine.

3. "There's too much of worriment goes in a bonnet;
   There's too much of ironing goes in a shirt.
   There's nothing that pays for the time you waste on it;
   There's nothing that lasts us but trouble and dirt.

4. "In March it is mud, it is snow in December;
   The mid-summer breezes are loaded with dust.
   In fall the leaves litter; in rainy September
   The wallpaper rots and the candlesticks rust.

5. "Last night in my dreams I was stationed forever
   On a far little isle in the midst of the sea.
   My one chance for life was a ceaseless endeavor
   To sweep off the waves ere they swept over me.

6. "Alas, 'twas no dream, for ahead I behold it;
   I know I am helpless my fate to avert."
   She put down her broom and her apron she folded,
   Then lay down and died, and was buried in dirt.

(over)

The old saying runs: "Man works from sun to sun, but woman's work is never done." The endless monotony of "woman's work" has seldom been more vividly described than in this house-wifely lament.

Keith Clark, recreation director in the town of Ottawa, Illinois, found the verses (called "The Housekeeper's Lament") in the diary of Mrs. Sara A. Price. Some of Mrs. Price's sons were killed in the Civil War, so the song apparently dates from the mid-nineteenth century. It also appears in nineteenth century songsters and was collected from a traditional singer in Florida. Its flavor is Irish, although it probably originated in the United States.

ACRES OF CLAMS

Words by FRANCIS D. HENRY

(over)

1. I've wandered all over this country
   Prospecting and digging for gold;
   I've tunneled, hydraulicked, and cradled,
   And I have been frequently sold.

   CHORUS: And I have been frequently sold,
            And I have been frequently sold—
            I've tunneled, hydraulicked, and cradled,
            And I have been frequently sold!

2. For one who got rich by mining
   I saw there were hundreds grew poor;
   I made up my mind to try farming,
   The only pursuit that is sure.

   CHORUS: The only pursuit that is sure,
            The only pursuit that is sure—
            I made up my mind to try farming,
            The only pursuit that is sure!

3. I rolled up my grub in my blanket,
   I left all my tools on the ground,
   I started one morning to shank it
   For the country they call Puget Sound.

   CHORUS: For the country they call Puget Sound,
            For the country they call Puget Sound—
            I started one morning to shank it
            For the country they call Puget Sound!

4. No longer the slave of ambition,
   I laugh at the world and its shams,
   And think of my happy condition
   Surrounded by acres of clams.

   CHORUS: Surrounded by acres of clams,
            Surrounded by acres of clams —
            And think of my happy condition
            Surrounded by acres of clams!

Sometimes called "The Old Settlers' Song," this ditty was the outcome of the frantic gold rushes of the nineteenth century. After flocking to California in 1849, many prospectors spent weary years wandering from strike to strike, hoping always that their luck would improve. Some ended up in South Dakota singing the lament of "The Dreary Black Hills." Those who had not been incurably bitten by the gold bug finally settled in the new western states and began to build up stable communities in place of the miners' ghost towns. This song, written by Judge Francis D. Henry, typifies their experiences.

Alan Lomax calls this "the best ballad we know from the Northwest." When the state of Washington was formed in 1889, it became the state song. The tune is Irish, used for the patriotic ballad, "Men of the West," and the comic ditty "Old Rosin the Beau." In the latter form it crossed to the States in 1838 and was used for many political parodies, the most important being the Republican campaign song, "Lincoln and Liberty."

THE TEACHER'S LAMENT

Music by MERLE TRAVIS

Forcefully

Some peo-ple say a tea-cher's made out of steel, Her mind can think, but her bo-dy can't feel; Iron and steel and hic-ko-ry tea, Frowns and gripes from nine to three. You teach six full hours and what do you get? A-no-ther day ol-der and dee-per in debt. You pay your dues in this and that Then for

CHORUS

no chords

(over)

twen-ty nine days your bill-fold's flat.

2. I   P. T. A.

2. I woke one morning, it was cloudy and cool
   I picked up my register and started for school,
   I wrote eighty-four names on the home room roll
   And the Principal said, "Well, bless my soul."

        You teach six full hours and what do you get?
        Cuts and bruises and dirt and sweat.
        I got two black eyes and can hardly walk.
        When I turned my back, then came the chalk.

3. I got eighty-four kids and forty-two seats—
   Sixty are talking, while twenty-four sleep.
   I can hardly get 'em all through the classroom door
   And if I don't watch out they'll give me twenty-four more.

        You teach six full hours to eighty-four brats
        And all of them yelling like dogs and cats.
        They're cutting on the seats and writing on the walls,
        Hugging and kissing in the upstairs halls.

4. The last bell rings and I start for the door,
   My head is ringing and my feet are sore.
   I taught six full hours — my day is made
   But I still have three hundred papers to grade.

        You teach six full hours and what do you get?
        Another day older and deeper in debt.
        I'll go to St. Peter, but I just can't stay—
        I gotta come back to the P.T.A.

The largest group of unorganized workers in the United States and Canada today consists of white-collar workers — school teachers, bank clerks, librarians, social workers, government employees, etc. Through their trade unions, industrial workers have improved their lot much faster than white-collar workers, and in many cases have left them far behind. In many cities the ordinary sweeper in a factory is getting a higher wage than college-trained school teachers.

The labor movement maintains that until white-collar workers organize into unions of their own they will continue to lag behind, and will be paid off in "prestige and position." However, "prestige" is hard to trade for food at the supermarket, as the "Teachers' Blues" suggests:

"Now unions are for workers, but a teacher has prestige.
He can feed his kids on that old noblesse oblige."

Scattered groups of professional and white-collar workers have organized effectively, and have even gone on strike. In 1956, insurance agents in Pennsylvania struck and told their employer:

"The company says we're professionals —
To this we'll always agree.
Until it comes up with more money,
Professional pickets we'll be!"

For many years teachers have been one of the most underpaid groups in society — and with the overcrowded classrooms of today they are also one of the most overworked. While "Sixteen Tons" was riding high on the hit parade, an Arkansas teacher was inspired to put her complaints into song, and verses like these were soon circulating throughout the country.

TOO OLD TO WORK

With steady rhythm

Words and music by JOE GLAZER

You work in the fac-to-ry all of your life, Try to pro-vide for your kids and your wife. When you get too old to pro-

(over)

144

2. You don't ask for favors when your life is through;
You've got a right to what's coming to you.
Your boss gets a pension when he is too old;
You helped him retire—you're out in the cold.

3. They put horses to pasture, they feed them on hay;
Even machines get retired some day.
The bosses get pensions when their days are through;
Fat pensions for them, brother; nothing for you.

4. There's no easy answer, there's no easy cure;
Dreaming won't change it, that's one thing for sure;
But fighting together we'll get there some day,
And when we have won we will no longer say:

In 1949 and 1950, the big industrial unions in the United States began a drive for company-paid pensions to supplement the inadequate government social security payments. The union slogan was "Too Old to Work, Too Young to Die."

Joe Glazer says he was moved to write this song after hearing Walter Reuther, President of the United Automobile Workers, make a speech blasting the double standard of the employers on the issue of pensions:

"I remember Reuther ripping into the automobile employers because out of one side of their mouths they attacked the unions' pension demands as 'creeping socialism,' while out of the other side of their mouths they stoutly defended their own huge company-paid pensions.

"I also remember Reuther telling this story of the mine mules that were used to pull the coal cars in his native West Virginia: 'During slack times the mules were put out to pasture. They were fed and kept healthy so they would be ready to work when the mine started up again. But did they put the coal miner out to pasture? Did they feed him and keep him healthy? They did not. And you know why? Because it cost fifty bucks to get another mule, but they could always get another coal miner for nothing.'

"Reuther's speech started the musical wheels turning in my head and a song started taking shape. However, it didn't get finished until some months later when the long pension strike of the Chrysler workers inspired me to write the final verses and to put the song into its present form."

AUTOMATION

Words and music by JOE GLAZER

I went down, down, down to the fac-to-ry Ear-ly on a Mon-day morn. When

I got down to the fac-to-ry It was lone-ly, it was for-lorn. I

could-n't find Joe, Jack, John, or Jim; No-bo-dy could I see:

No-thing but but-tons and bells and lights All o-ver the fac-to-ry.

2. I walked, walked, walked into the foreman's office
   To find out what was what.
   I looked him in the eye and I said, "What goes?"
   And this is the answer I got:
   His eyes turned red, then green, then blue
   And it suddenly dawned on me—
   There was a robot sitting in the seat
   Where the foreman used to be.

3. I walked all around, all around, up and down
   And across that factory.
   I watched all the buttons and the bells and the lights—
   It was a mystery to me.
   I hollered "Frank, Hank, Ike, Mike, Roy, Ray, Don, Dan,
   Bill, Phil, Ed, Fred, Pete!"
   And a great big mechanical voice boomed out:
   "All your buddies are obsolete."

4. I was scared, scared, scared, I was worried, I was sick
   As I left that factory.
   I decided that I had to see the president
   Of the whole darn company.
   When I got up to his office he was rushing out the door
   With a scowl upon his face,
   'Cause there was a great big mechanical executive
   Sitting in the president's place.

5. I went home, home, home to my ever-loving wife
   And told her 'bout the factory.
   She hugged me and she kissed me and she cried a little bit
   As she sat on my knee.
   I don't understand all the buttons and the lights
   But one thing I will say—
   I thank the Lord that love's still made
   In the good old-fashioned way.

Factories without workers? Machines without men? Offices without office girls? Fantastic! Yet the numerous examples of "automation," called by many the Second Industrial Revolution, make these predictions not fantastic at all. We now have machines that give orders to other machines; machines that "think" and correct their own mistakes; machines that translate foreign languages; machines that play checkers—and win.

The computers that predict the orbits of man-made satellites can make 42,000 mathematical calculations a second. One government check-writing machine can turn out 80,000 checks a day. A certain type of electronic computing machine can do the work of about a hundred conventional tabulating-machine operators. A completely automatic plant producing concrete can load into ready-mix trucks any one of some 1,500 different mixing formulas—without using any manual labor.

"Labor welcomes these technological changes," says AFL-CIO President George Meany. "The new techniques offer promise of higher living standards for all, greater leisure, and more pleasant working conditions. Yet there are pitfalls as well as promises in the new technology. There is no automatic guarantee that the potential benefits to society will be transformed into reality. While the new machines are almost human in the way they solve problems of production, they still cannot create the necessary income to purchase their additional output."

Joe Glazer's song, "Automation," seems light-hearted and humorous, but it reflects the concern and fear most workers have of the new technological age.

THE RICH MAN AND THE POOR MAN

Glo - ry hal - le lu - jah, hi - ro - je - rum.

2. One day to his door there came a human wreckium,
   Glory hallelujah, hi-ro-jerum.
   He wore a bowler hat and the brim was round his neckium,
   Glory hallelujah, hi-ro-jerum.

3. The poor man begged for a piece of bread and cheesium,
   Glory hallelujah, hi-ro-jerum.
   The rich man said he'd call for a policium,
   Glory hallelujah, hi-ro-jerum.

4. The poor man died, and his soul went to Heavium,
   Glory hallelujah, hi-ro-jerum.
   He danced with the angels till a quarter past elevium,
   Glory hallelujah, hi-ro-jerum.

5. The rich man died, but he didn't fare so wellium,
   Glory hallelujah, hi-ro-jerum.
   He couldn't get to Heaven, so he had to go to Hellium,
   Glory hallelujah, hi-ro-jerum.

6. The moral of this story is: Riches are no jokium,
   Glory hallelujah, hi-ro-jerum.
   We'll all go to Heaven 'cause we're all stony brokium,
   Glory hallelujah, hi-ro-jerum.

The Biblical parable of Dives and Lazarus has always been a favorite among working people. Dives, the rich man, had all he wanted on earth, while Lazarus, the poor man, begged for crumbs at his door. But when they died Lazarus "was carried by the angels into Abraham's bosom," while the rich man, in Hell, begged for a drop of water to quench his burning thirst (Luke 16:19).

Many centuries ago the English peasants turned this story into a carol, and it has been handed down to our time. In 1557, Master John Wallye and Mistress Toye paid a license fee to the Company of Stationers for printing a "Ballad of the Ryche man and poor Lazarus," and one of Fletcher's plays printed in 1639 refers to the "merry ballad of Diverus and Lazarus." It appears in the great ballad collection of Francis James Child as Number 56.

The original carol followed the Bible story closely and was sung very seriously. Later the Negroes told the story in a spiritual:

"Rich man Dives he lived so well,
When he died he found a home in hell;
Poor man Lazarus, poor as I,
When he died he had a home on high."

In more recent times the tale was re-told in a light-hearted vein and became popular among college students and community song groups. This modern parody of the ancient English carol was included in a songbook published by the Brookwood Labor College, one of the earliest American schools for workers, which was established in 1921 in Katonah, New York.

THE DODGER

Satirically

Oh, the can-di-date's a dod-ger, yes, a well known dod-ger, Oh, the
can-di-date's a dod-ger, yes, and I'm a dod-ger too. He'll meet you and treat you and
ask you for your vote, But look out, boys, he's a- dod-ging for a note! Oh, we're
all dod-ging, a- dod-ging, dod-ging, dod-ging, Oh, we're all dod-ging our way thru' the world.

1. Oh, the candidate's a dodger, yes, a well-known dodger,
   Oh, the candidate's a dodger, yes, and I'm a dodger, too.
   He'll meet you and treat you and ask you for your vote,
   But look out, boys, he's a-dodging for a note!

CHORUS: Oh, we're all dodging, a-dodging, dodging, dodging,
          Oh, we're all dodging our way through the world.

2. Oh, the lawyer he's a dodger, yes, a well-known dodger,
   Oh, the lawyer he's a dodger, yes, and I'm a dodger, too.
   He'll plead your case and claim you for a friend,
   But look out boys, he's easy for to bend!

3. Oh, the preacher he's a dodger, yes, a well-known dodger,
   Oh, the preacher he's a dodger, yes, and I'm a dodger, too.
   He'll preach you the gospel and tell you of your crimes,
   But look out, boys, he's a-dodging for your dimes!

4. Oh, the merchant he's a dodger, yes, a well-known dodger,
   Oh, the merchant he's a dodger, yes, and I'm a dodger, too.
   He'll sell you goods at double the price
   And when you go to pay him, you'll have to pay him twice!

5. Oh, the farmer he's a dodger, yes, a well-known dodger,
   Oh, the farmer he's a dodger, yes, and I'm a dodger, too.
   He'll plow his cotton, he'll hoe his corn,
   And he'll make a living just as sure as you're born!

6. Oh, the lover he's a dodger, yes, a well-known dodger,
   Oh, the lover he's a dodger, yes, and I'm a dodger, too.
   He'll hug you and kiss you and call you his bride,
   But look out, girls, he's a-telling you a lie!

Like "The Farmer Is The Man," "The Dodger" originated with the Western farmers during the period of agrarian protest following the Civil War. It is linked specifically with the presidential election of 1884 when the Democratic candidate, Grover Cleveland, was running against Republican James Blaine. Cleveland had won the support of progressives by his fight against Tammany Hall in New York, and "The Dodger" was apparently used as a campaign song to belittle Blaine. The version known today is based on a Library of Congress recording by Mrs. Emma Dusenberry of Mena, Arkansas, who learned it in the 1880's. It was transcribed and first published by Charles Seeger in a little Resettlement Administration songbook.

NO IRISH NEED APPLY

Words by J. F. POOLE

I'm a de-cent boy just lan-ded from the town of Bal-ly-fad; I
seen em-ploy-ment ad-ver-tised, "It's just the thing," says I, But the

want a si-tu-a-tion and I want it ve-ry bad. I have
dir-ty spal-peen en-ded with "No

I-rish need ap-ply." "Whoo," says I, that is an in-sult, but to get the place I'll

try," So I went to see the black-guard with his "No I-rish need ap-

rit. - - - -

2. I started out to find the house; I got there mighty soon.
   I found the old chap seated; he was reading the Tribune.
   I told him what I came for, when he in a rage did fly.
   "No!" he says, "You are a Paddy, and no Irish need apply."
   Then I gets my dander rising, and I'd like to black his eye
   For to tell an Irish gentleman "No Irish Need Apply."
3. I couldn't stand it longer so a-hold of him I took,
   And I gave him such a beating as he'd get at Donnybrook,
   He hollered "Milia Murther," and to get away did try,
   And swore he'd never write again "No Irish Need Apply."
   Well, he made a big apology; I told him then goodbye,
   Saying, "When next you want a beating, write 'No Irish Need Apply.'"

During the nineteenth century, America was the land of opportunity to poverty-stricken families of many countries — but all too often the immigrants who came here looking for work found that their services were not wanted. Their color, race, language, or religion was made the excuse for barring them from jobs. At different times and in different places the bars went up against Irish, Jews, Poles, Italians, Japanese, and even English.

The potato famines of 1845-7 led thousands of Irishmen to flee their starving country. Soon American cities were flooded with immigrants living in slum ghettos, and employers were posting "No Irish Need Apply" signs.

This song, which has been revived by Peter Seeger, was popular in nineteenth-century music halls. It was written around 1865 and printed in several song books of that period. A somewhat similar song, "No Irish Wanted Here," passed into oral tradition in both the United States and Canada.

Ballyfadd, in the first line, is a small town in southeastern Ireland near Arklow. "The Tribune" mentioned in the second verse probably was the famous nineteenth-century paper edited by Horace Greeley. "Milia murther" in the last verse seems to be based on a Gaelic phrase meaning "a thousand murders."

TIMES IS MIGHTY HARD

From "The American Songbag" by Carl Sandburg.
Pub. by Harcourt and Brace. Used by permission.

Note from Carl Sandburg: *The American Songbag*

"This little croon is an impromptu, made up in some hour when a man or woman holding a baby, or rocking a cradle, needed hushing words for a hushing tune. Of course, the statistical information that a dollar a day is all they pay for work on the boulevard does not interest a sleepy child, but as crooned by Robert E. Lee of the *Chicago Tribune*, the word 'boul-e-vard' has a comforting and soothing quality. Lee heard the song from an Irishman in charge of the railroad station at Wallingford, Iowa. While selling passenger tickets, or making out way-bills, or figuring freight demurrage, or hustling trunks off and on baggage cars, or piling crates of eggs, 'the agent' would ease his heart with this lullaby."

THE PREACHER AND THE SLAVE

Words by JOE HILL

(over)

1. Long-haired preachers come out ev'ry night,
   Try to tell you what's wrong and what's right,
   But when asked about something to eat,
   They will answer with voices so sweet:

CHORUS: You will eat (you will eat), bye and bye (bye and bye),
   In that glorious land in the sky (way up high).
   Work and pray (work and pray), live on hay (live on hay),
   You'll get pie in the sky when you die (that's a lie!).

2. And the starvation army they play,
   And they sing and they clap and they pray,
   Till they get all your coin on the drum—
   Then they tell you when you're on the bum:

3. If you fight hard for children and wife—
   Try to get something good in this life—
   You're a sinner and bad man, they tell;
   When you die you will sure go to Hell.

4. Working men of all countries, unite!
   Side by side we for freedom will fight.
   When the world and its wealth we have gained,
   To the grafters we'll sing this refrain:

LAST CHORUS:
   You will eat (you will eat), bye and bye, (bye and bye),
   When you've learned how to cook and to fry (way up high).
   Chop some wood (chop some wood)—'twill do you good (do you good)
   And you'll eat in the sweet bye and bye (that's no lie!).

How did the Industrial Workers of the World get the nickname "Wobbly"? We do not really know. One story has it originating with a Chinese cook on a railroad gang. When he was signed up during an IWW drive, he proudly proclaimed his membership in the organization, but when he spoke the initials, they came out: "I Wobbly Wobbly."

Whatever the true origin, Wobbly was the common designation for those rebels-against-society who made up America's most colorful and revolutionary union — the spokesmen of the dispossessed and the disinherited, the "have-nots" of a rich continent.

More important to the Wobblies than building up regular trade unions was their battle against the "haves" and against the system which they fiercely believed exploited them and the mass of mankind. The famous preamble to the IWW constitution opened with these words:

> "The working class and the employing class have nothing in common . . . Between these classes a struggle must go on until the workers of the world organize as a class, take possession of the earth and the machinery of production, and abolish the wage system."

The IWW concentrated much of their efforts on organizing the migratory and casual laborers of the lumber and construction camps. In between jobs these migrants would gather in the Skid Rows of Chicago, Portland, Seattle and other cities they used as a "base of operations." There on the street corners was the inevitable Salvation Army band anxious to save lost Wobbly souls.

But the Wobblies were more interested in filling their stomachs than in saving their souls, and they ridiculed the Salvation Army hymns with biting parodies aimed at what came to be known as "pie in the sky" preaching. Thus the gospel hymn, "What a Friend We Have in Jesus," became "Dump the Bosses Off Your Back"; "There Is Power in the Blood of the Lamb" was changed to "There is Power in a Union," and so on.

The most successful of these parodies was Joe Hill's masterpiece, "The Preacher and the Slave," more widely known as "Pie in the Sky" — a devastating take-off on the hymn, "Sweet Bye and Bye." It quickly became part of folk tradition, and a dozen years after Joe Hill's death Carl Sandburg included it in his *American Songbag*.

The Wobbly songs based on hymns reflect their strong anti-clerical bias. It is interesting to note the strong contrast between these and the many fine labor songs using hymn tunes which preserve the spirit of the original — for example, "We Shall Not Be Moved," "We Will Overcome," or "We Are Building a Strong Union."

THE MAN THAT WATERS THE WORKER'S BEER

Words by PADDY RYAN

I'm the man, the ve-ry fat man, that wa-ters the wor-kers' beer.—— Yes,

I'm the man, the ve-ry fat man, that wa-ters the wor-kers' beer.—— What

do I care if it makes them ill, or it makes them ter-rib-ly queer? I've a

car, a yacht, and an aer-o plane, and I wa-ters the wor-kers' beer. Now beer.

CHORUS: I'm the man, the very fat man
That waters the workers' beer.
Yes, I'm the man, the very fat man
That waters the workers' beer.
What do I care if it makes them ill,
Or it makes them terribly queer?
I've a car, a yacht, and an aeroplane,
And I waters the workers' beer.

1. When I makes the workers' beer
I puts in strychinine,
Some methylated spirits
And a drop of paraffin.
But since a brew so terribly strong
Might make them terribly queer,
I reaches my hand for the water tap
And I waters the workers' beer.

2. A drop of good beer is good for a man
Who's thirsty, tired, and hot,
And sometimes I has a drop for myself
From a very special lot;
But a fat and healthy working class
Is the thing that I most fear,
So I reaches my hand for the water tap
And I waters the workers' beer.

3. Now ladies fair, beyond compare,
Be ye maid or wife,
Oh, sometimes lend a thought for one
Who leads a wand'ring life.
The water rates are shockingly high
And chemicals are so dear,
So there isn't the profit there used to be
When I water the workers' beer.

This satirical ditty comes from England. The tune is based on the traditional Irish song, "The Son of a Gambolier," and the words were written by Paddy Ryan. It was first printed by the British Workers' Music Association in 1939, and appears in the *Labour Party Song Book* published in 1955.

I DON'T WANT YOUR MILLIONS, MISTER

Words by JIM GARLAND

1. I don't want your millions, mister;
   I don't want your diamond ring.
   All I want is the right to live, mister;
   Give me back my job again.

2. I don't want your Rolls-Royce, mister;
   I don't want your pleasure yacht;
   All I want is food for my babies;
   Give to me my old job back.

3. We worked to build this country, mister,
   While you enjoyed a life of ease;
   You've stolen all that we built, mister;
   Now our children starve and freeze.

4. Think me dumb if you wish, mister;
   Call me green or blue or red;
   This one thing I sure know, mister:
   My hungry babies must be fed.

5. I don't want your millions, mister,
   I don't want your diamond ring.
   All I want is the right to live, mister;
   Give me back my job again.

This song was written in 1932 during the dark days of the coal mining wars in Harlan County, Kentucky (See Page 55). The tune is that of an old love song known as "East Virginia" or "Greenback Dollars."

Jim Garland, the author, was a younger brother of Aunt Molly Jackson, a union stalwart who composed many ballads about the miners' struggles. Garland himself was a coal miner who had been blacklisted for union activity.

The song became more widely known when the Almanac singers recorded it in 1941. Woody Guthrie always insisted they were insincere in singing it: "If we'd only admit it, we do want the man's millions and diamond ring and his yacht and everything else."

SONG OF THE GUARANTEED WAGE

Words by RUBY McDONALD and JOE GLAZER

I'll tell you the sto-ry of Jo-na-thon Tweed, Who had a good wife and four chil-dren to feed. His wa-ges bought food and a place they could bunk, But dur-ing a lay-off, poor John-ny was sunk. Yes, sunk

2. When Johnny was working he'd get along fine
   But when he was laid off he'd worry and pine.
   He did not get paid, but his bills did not cease,
   No wonder poor Johnny could not sleep in peace.
   No wonder poor Johnny could not sleep in peace.

3. Now, Jonathan Tweed said there must be a way
   To guarantee workers a regular pay.
   And that's when he thought of a guaranteed plan
   And the boys in the union backed him to a man.
   The boys in the union backed him to a man.

4. Said Jonathan Tweed, now there's one thing quite queer:
   The bosses get paid every week in the year,
   But now when we ask for a guaranteed wage
   They rant and they roar and break out in a rage.
   Yes, they rant and they roar and break out in a rage.

5. Now, wife, if we win it, our future is clear,
   We'll draw up our budget with confidence, dear.
   And children, at last you can live unafraid,
   When you know that your daddy will always get paid.
   You'll know that your daddy will always get paid.

6. Come all of you workers, pray listen, take heed,
   For this is the message of Jonathan Tweed:
   Though big corporations may bellow and rage,
   We'll stand up and fight for a guaranteed wage.
   Yes, we'll stand and we'll fight for a guaranteed wage.

From the beginnings of the Industrial Revolution the factory worker has been haunted by the fear of unemployment. His tools were no longer his own; he was completely dependent upon the boss; without a job, how could he feed his children, how could he keep his family together?

Unemployment destroys a worker's dignity and self-respect. It brings gnawing worry, fear, and despair. It can ruin a man's future, destroy his whole life. "The saddest object in civilization," said Robert Louis Stevenson, "and the greatest confession of its failure, is the man who can work and wants to work, and is not allowed to work."

Small wonder, then, that unions for the past hundred and fifty years have been seriously concerned about the long series of panics, depressions, and recessions that have plagued our economy.

The first important milestone in the workers' battle against insecurity was the adoption of unemployment insurance in the 1930's. In the 1950's another great step forward was made when the guaranteed annual wage, or guaranteed employment plans, were incorporated into many union contracts.

The campaign for the G.A.W. was spearheaded by the powerful auto workers' union, the UAW. The plan was developed in 1954 and 1955 and reached a climax at the UAW Convention in April, 1955. Joe Glazer reports:

> "At the request of UAW leaders, I tried for months to write a G.A.W. song which could be used in the campaign, but I could not get it to come out right. Then just before the UAW Convention, Ruby McDonald, the talented wife of a Flint auto worker, sent me a song which had exactly the right feel. I worked it over a bit and came up with the 'Song of the Guaranteed Wage,' set to the tune of 'Sweet Betsy From Pike.' I introduced it to the twenty-five hundred delegates at the Convention and it was received enthusiastically."

In an historic down-to-the-wire battle with the Ford Corporation, the UAW won a form of the G.A.W. without a strike in 1955. Soon after, unions in steel, rubber, glass, and other industries won similar guarantees in their contracts. Those plans, usually called "Supplemental Unemployment Benefits" (S.U.B.), are still being extended and improved to provide greater security for the worker.

164

OH, FREEDOM

1. No more moaning, no more moaning,
   No more moaning, Lord, for me!
   And before I'd be a slave, I'd be buried in my grave,
   And go home to my Lord and be free.

2. No more crying, no more crying,
   No more crying, Lord, for me!
   And before I'd be a slave, I'd be buried in my grave,
   And go home to my Lord and be free.

3. O freedom! O freedom!
   O freedom, Lord, for me!
   And before I'd be a slave, I'd be buried in my grave,
   And go home to my Lord and be free.

The Negroes were by no means submissive under the intolerable conditions of slavery. It is not generally known that there were over a hundred slave revolts in the United States during the eighteenth and nineteenth centuries. Most of these uprisings were small and ineffectual, but that the Negroes should so often have risked brutal retaliation to strike for freedom is convincing proof of their hatred of bondage. From this hatred sprang the stirring spiritual which later became the marching song of Negro regiments in the Civil War. Its powerful phrases make it a moving plea for the freedom of oppressed peoples everywhere.

WE ARE MARCHING ON TO VICTORY

(over)

1. We are marching on to vict'ry,
   We are marching on to vict'ry,
   We are marching on to vict'ry
      With hope and dignity.

2. We shall all stand together,
   We shall all stand together,
   We shall all stand together
      'Till everyone is free.

3. We know love is the watchword,
   We know love is the watchword,
   We know love is the watchword
      For peace and liberty.

4. Black and white all are brothers,
   Black and white all are brothers,
   Black and white all are brothers
      To live in harmony.

Although nearly a hundred years have passed since Lincoln abolished slavery, the Negroes in the Southern states are not yet completely free. The bitterness that came out of the Civil War found expression in many forms of discrimination: legal, economic, and social, which have continued to deny the Negroes full citizenship.

The battle against Jim Crow has been fought on many fronts, and little by little the victory is being won. One of the most important decisions in that fight came on May 17, 1954, when the judges of the Supreme Court ruled unanimously that racial segregation in public schools of the United States was unconstitutional. That decision is still being fought out in many local engagements, but there is reason to hope that it indicates the shape of things to come.

Less far-reaching but equally significant is the victory that was won in 1956 in the city of Montgomery, Alabama. The engagement started on December 1, 1955, when the driver of a Montgomery City Lines bus asked Mrs. Rosa Parkes to give up her seat to a white person. Mrs. Parkes refused, was arrested, and fined $10 and costs. That was the spark that set off a spontaneous strike against the bus line which had already built up a bitter backlog of hatred by its harsh treatment of the Negro passengers who made up 70 per cent of its patrons.

Under the leadership of two dozen Negro ministers, the Montgomery Improvement Association was formed with Rev. Martin Luther King as its leader, and the bus boycott took permanent shape. Volunteers offered the use of their cars; mass-meeting collections furnished funds to buy twenty station wagons to drive workers to their jobs; when no other means could be found, they walked.

Through a long year the struggle continued. Martin King's home was bombed; many of the strike leaders were indicted on charges of violating a 1921 anti-boycott law; officials took the Montgomery Improvement League to court on the charge of setting up an illegal transport system. Through all provocations and obstacles the Negroes held quietly to their course, maintaining discipline, avoiding violence — and staying off the buses. They held out until November, 1956, when the U. S. Supreme Court declared bus segregation illegal in Montgomery.

Through the year-long boycott, frequent meetings were held in the churches, and singing played a big part in keeping up the strikers' morale. They sang the old hymns and spirituals with great intensity, and created some new ones, like "We Are Marching On To Victory," set to the tune of the well-known spiritual, "Give Me That Old-Time Religion."

Mrs. Eleanor Roosevelt has saluted the victory in these words: "The bus protest carried on by the colored people of Montgomery, Alabama, without violence, has been one of the most remarkable achievements of people fighting for their rights but doing so without bloodshed and with the most remarkable restraint and discipline that we have ever witnessed in this country."

THE ABOLITIONIST HYMN

1. We ask not that the slave should lie
   As lies his master, at his ease,
   Beneath a silken canopy
   Or in the shade of blooming trees.

2. We ask not "eye for eye," that all
   Who forge the chain and ply the whip
   Should feel their torture, while the thrall
   Should wield the scourge of mastership.

3. We mourn not that the man should toil;
   'Tis nature's need, 'tis God's decree;
   But let the hand that tills the soil
   Be, like the wind that fans it, free.

During the years just before the American Civil War when the tension between the North and South was growing, both white and black men began to sing of the day when slavery would be no more. The leaders of the Abolitionist movement set up anti-slavery singing circles and wrote special songs for them, generally set to the tune of old hymns. The best of them was this "Abolitionist Hymn" set to the familiar "Old Hundred."

GO DOWN, MOSES

1. When Israel was in Egypt's land,
      Let my people go!
   Oppressed so hard they could not stand,
      Let my people go!

CHORUS: "Go down Moses,
            'Way down in Egypt's land,
            Tell old Pharoah
            To let my people go!"

2. "Thus spoke the Lord," bold Moses said,
      "Let my people go!
   If not, I'll smite your firstborn dead,
      Let my people go!"

3. "No more shall they in bondage toil,
      Let my people go!
   Let them come out with Egypt's spoil,
      Let my people go!"

Some of the noblest songs of freedom were composed by Negro slaves. In their spirituals they naturally chose for their heroes little David who slew the mighty Goliath; Daniel, whom the Lord delivered from the lions, and Joshua, who made the walls come tumbling down. In the trials and tribulations of the children of Israel they saw the pattern of their own bondage. Thus they could do full justice to one of the great Bible stories of liberation: the story of Moses who stood up to Pharoah and said: "Let my people go!"

In the years before the Civil War many slaves were guided along the Underground Railroad by an escaped slave called Harriet Tubman. She was called the Moses of her people because she led them out of bondage, and it is said that the Negroes made this song in her honor. Later it was sung by Negro regiments in the Civil War.

In the summer of 1957 Joe Glazer was in Israel and recalls hearing this song under unusual circumstances.

"It was in the city of Haifa on the top of Mt. Carmel. I had been asked to sing that night with a chorus of Israeli army officers. I was a little late and they had already started singing. It was powerful and strange — the Negro spiritual, 'Go Down, Moses,' sung in Hebrew!

"This story of Pharoah and the children of Israel had indeed made a strange cycle. White Christians brought the story of the Bible to the New World. Negro slaves, carried thousands of miles across the ocean, learned the ancient story of the bondage of the children of Israel and shaped it into a song reflecting their own hopes for freedom. Several hundred years later the song travels back across the ocean to the land of the Bible itself, is translated into the Hebrew of the Old Testament, and sung by the Jews who had returned from the four corners of the earth to the land of their fathers."

The song was especially apt just then because the Israeli soldiers had recently returned with "Egypt's spoil" — tanks, guns, ammunition — taken from General Nasser's army in the Sinai campaign of 1956.

JOHN BROWN'S BODY

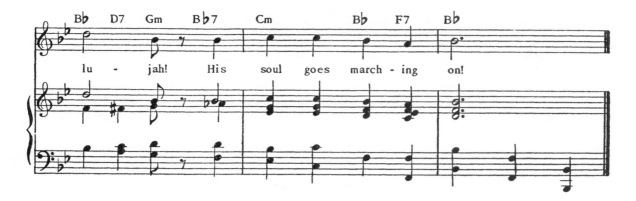

lu - jah! His soul goes march - ing on!

1. John Brown's body lies a-mould'ring in the grave,
   John Brown's body lies a-mould'ring in the grave,
   John Brown's body lies a-mould'ring in the grave,
   But his soul goes marching on.

CHORUS: Glory, glory, hallelujah!
   Glory, glory, hallelujah!
   Glory, glory, hallelujah!
   His soul goes marching on!

2. John Brown died that the slaves might be free,
   John Brown died that the slaves might be free,
   John Brown died that the slaves might be free,
   But his soul goes marching on.

3. He captured Harper's Ferry with his nineteen men so true;
   He frightened Old Virginny till she trembled through and through;
   They hung him for a traitor, themselves the traitor crew,
   But his soul is marching on.

4. He's gone to be a soldier in the army of the Lord,
   He's gone to be a soldier in the army of the Lord,
   He's gone to be a soldier in the army of the Lord,
   His soul is marching on.

5. The stars of Heaven now are looking kindly down,
   The stars of Heaven now are looking kindly down,
   The stars of Heaven now are looking kindly down,
   On the grave of old John Brown.

The tune that has been used for three of America's most famous songs — "John Brown's Body," "The Battle Hymn of the Republic," and "Solidarity Forever" — began life as a camp-meeting hymn called "Say Brothers Will You Meet Us?" written by a Southern composer, William Steffe, in the middle 1850's. That hymn with its "Glory Hallelujah" refrain became quite popular with the Twelfth Massachusetts Regiment stationed at Fort Warren in Boston Harbor, and it was there that the "John Brown" parody is said to have originated.

It was in 1859 that John Brown led a little party of twenty-five men against the garrison at Harper's Ferry in a quixotic attempt to capture arms and liberate the slaves. The pitiful little force was routed, Brown's two sons were killed, and he himself was captured. When Colonel Robert E. Lee asked him his purpose and by what authority he had acted, John Brown replied: "To free the slaves — by the authority of God Almighty." He was tried by the State of Virginia on the charge of treason, and in his defense before the court he said:

(over)

"This court acknowledges, as I suppose, the validity of the law of God. I believe that to have interfered as I have done, in behalf of His despised poor, was not wrong but right. Now if it be deemed necessary that I should mingle my blood further with the blood of my children and with the millions in this slave country whose rights are disregarded by wicked, cruel, and unjust enactments, I submit. So let it be done!"

John Brown was hanged on December 2, 1859, but, like other martyrs, he accomplished more by his death than by his life. He became a hero throughout the North, and when the Civil War broke out, "John Brown's Body" became the favorite marching song of the Union soldiers.

Some of the early verses were much more elaborate than the simple three-line repetitions which have survived. A volume of *The Christy Minstrels' Favorite Songs* gave the first verse in this form:

"Old John Brown's body lies a-mould'ring in the grave,
While weep the sons of bondage whom he ventur'd all to save,
But though he lost his life in struggling for the slaves,
His soul is marching on."

THE BATTLE HYMN OF THE REPUBLIC

1. Mine eyes have seen the glory of the coming of the Lord;
   He is trampling out the vintage where the grapes of wrath are stored;
   He hath loosed the fateful lightning of His terrible swift sword:
   His truth is marching on.

CHORUS: Glory, glory hallelujah
   Glory, glory hallelujah
   Glory, glory hallelujah
   His truth is marching on.

2. I have seen Him in the watch-fires of a hundred circling camps;
   They have builded Him an altar in the evening dews and damps;
   I can read His righteous sentence by the dim and flaring lamps;
   His day is marching on.

3. I have read a fiery gospel, writ in burnished rows of steel;
   "As ye deal with My contemners, so with you My grace shall deal;
   Let the Hero, born of woman, crush the serpent with his heel,
   Since God is marching on."

4. He has sounded forth the trumpet that shall never call retreat;
   He is sifting out the hearts of men before His judgment-seat;
   Oh, be swift, my soul, to answer Him! be jubilant, my feet!
   Our God is marching on.

5. In the beauty of the lilies Christ was born across the sea,
   With a glory in His bosom that transfigures you and me:
   As He died to make men holy, let us die to make men free,
   While God is marching on.

One night in December, 1861, Julia Ward Howe sat in her hotel room in Washington listening to the regiments sing "John Brown's Body" as they marched to the front. From her window she could see the camp fires of the Union Army, and as she watched them a poem began to form in her mind. She wrote it down on a scrap of paper, and a couple of months later it was published in *The Atlantic Monthly*. Thus the stirring "Battle Hymn of the Republic" came into existence.

NO MORE AUCTION BLOCK FOR ME

1. No more auction block for me,
   No more, no more!
   No more auction block for me;
   Many thousand gone.

2. No more driver's lash for me,
   No more, no more!
   No more driver's lash for me;
   Many thousand gone.

3. No more peck of corn for me,
   No more, no more!
   No more peck of corn for me;
   Many thousand gone.

4. No more pint of salt for me,
   No more, no more!
   No more pint of salt for me;
   Many thousand gone.

This anthem of liberation probably dates from "the Year of Jubilo." On January 1, 1863, Lincoln's Emancipation Proclamation came into effect. Soon many of the Negroes he had set free were fighting with the Union forces, and as they marched they sang the thrilling lines of "No More Auction Block For Me."

The "pint of salt" and "peck of corn" were slavery rations. From a speech delivered in 1862 comes this comment:

"I asked one of these blacks where they got these songs. 'Dey make 'em, sah!' How do they make them? I'll tell you, it's dis way. My master calls me up and order me a short peck of corn and a hundred lash. My friends see it, and is sorry for me. When dey come to de praise-meeting dat night dey sing about it. Some's very good singers and know how; and dey work it in — work it in, you know, till they get it right; and dat's de way!'"

THESE THINGS SHALL BE

Words by JOHN ADDINGTON SYMONDS

1. These things shall be; a loftier race
   Than e'er the world hath known shall rise,
   With flame of freedom in their souls
   And light of knowledge in their eyes.

2. They shall be gentle, brave, and strong
   To spill no drop of blood, but dare
   All that may plant man's lordship firm
   On earth, and fire, and sea, and air.

3. Nation with nation, land with land,
   Unarmed shall live as comrades free;
In every heart and brain shall throb
   The pulse of one fraternity.

4. Man shall love man with heart as pure
   And fervent as the young-eyed throng
Who chant their heavenly psalm before
   God's face with undiscordant song.

5. New arts shall bloom of loftier mould,
   And mightier music thrill the skies,
And every life shall be a song,
   When all the earth is paradise.

6. There shall be no more sin, nor shame,
   Though pain and passion may not die;
For man shall be at one with God
   In bonds of firm necessity.

One of the best expressions of man's yearning for a nobler world, this well-known hymn was written by the Victorian poet and essayist, John Addington Symonds (1840-1893). In his own day, Symonds was famous for his seven-volume work, *The Renaissance in Italy,* but these brief verses are likely to outlive that monumental classic.

THE CUTTY WREN

As a ritual

"Oh, where are you go - ing?" said Mil - der to Mal - der, "Oh, we may not tell you," said Fest - le to Fose. "We're

(over)

1. "Oh, where are you going?" said Milder to Malder;
   "Oh, we may not tell you," said Festle to Fose.
   "We're off to the woods," said John the Red Nose.
   "We're off to the woods," said John the Red Nose.

2. "What will you do there?" said Milder to Malder;
   "Oh, we may not tell you," said Festle to Fose.
   "We'll shoot the Cutty Wren," said John the Red Nose.
   "We'll shoot the Cutty Wren," said John the Red Nose.

3. "How will you shoot her?" said Milder to Malder;
   "Oh, we may not tell you," said Festle to Fose.
   "With bows and with arrows," said John the Red Nose.
   "With bows and with arrows," said John the Red Nose.

4. "That will not do," said Milder to Malder;
   "Oh, what will do then?" said Festle to Fose.
   "Big guns and big cannons," said John the Red Nose.
   "Big guns and big cannons," said John the Red Nose.

5. "How will you bring her home?" said Milder to Malder;
   "Oh, we may not tell you," said Festle to Fose.
   "On four strong men's shoulders," said John the Red Nose.
   "On four strong men's shoulders," said John the Red Nose.

6. "That will not do," said Milder to Malder;
   "What will do then?" said Festle to Fose.
   "Big carts and big wagons," said John the Red Nose.
   "Big carts and big wagons," said John the Red Nose.

7. "How will you cut her up?" said Milder to Malder;
   "Oh, we may not tell you," said Festle to Fose.
   "With knives and with forks," said John the Red Nose.
   "With knives and with forks," said John the Red Nose.

8. "That will not do," said Milder to Malder;
   "What will do then?" said Festle to Fose.
   "Big hatchets and cleavers," said John the Red Nose.
   "Big hatchets and cleavers," said John the Red Nose.

9. "Oh, how will you cook her?" said Milder to Malder;
   "Oh, we may not tell you," said Festle to Fose.
   "With pots and with pans," said John the Red Nose.
   "With pots and with pans," said John the Red Nose.

10. "Oh, that will not do," said Milder to Malder;
    "What will do then?" said Festle to Fose.
    "Bloody great brass cauldrons," said John the Red Nose.
    "Bloody great brass cauldrons," said John the Red Nose.

11. "And who'll get the spare-ribs?" said Milder to Malder;
    "Oh, we may not tell you," said Festle to Fose.
    "We'll give them all to the poor," said John the Red Nose.
    "We'll give them all to the poor," said John the Red Nose.

"The Cutty Wren" dates back to the Peasants' Revolt of 1381. That was the time when baronial oppression caused widespread mutterings among the common people of England, and many of them began to meet in secret to plan the overthrow of their masters.

The symbolism of the song grew out of the old pagan custom of hunting the wren. In many legends, the wren, known as "King of the Birds," is pictured as a tyrant, and throughout the Middle Ages there were annual ceremonies surrounding the killing of the wren. Describing the ceremony held on Christmas Eve on the Isle of Man, A. L. Lloyd writes in *The Singing Englishman*:

> "Whether the masters liked it or not, the servants would all take the day off to go to church, and when the bells rang at midnight they would set off to hunt the wren. When they caught one, they killed it, put it on a long pole with its wings extended, and carried it in procession to every house. For a few hours till dawn they had the freedom of the village and they could do pretty well as they pleased, even in the master's house."

Apparently, the "King Wren" became a symbol of baronial property, and this song was probably sung at secret meetings when the peasants were planning to seize and redistribute the land among the poor. Its rebellious symbolism survived to the present century, for an old English shepherd who sang it stamped violently when he reached the last line, declaring that it was a defiant song and that to stamp was "the right way, and reminds you of the old times."

In later days, the symbolism of "The Cutty Wren" was forgotten, and it was transformed into a popular children's ditty, "Billy Barlow."

DIE GEDANKEN SIND FREI

Translation by ARTHUR KEVESS

Die Ge-dan-ken sind frei, my thoughts free-ly flo-wer, Die Ge-dan-ken sind frei, my thoughts give me po-wer, No scho-lar can map them, no hun-ter can trap them, No man can de-ny: Die Ge-dan-ken sind frei. No man can de-ny, Die Ge-dan-ken sind frei!

1. Die Gedanken sind frei, my thoughts freely flower,
   Die Gedanken sind frei, my thoughts give me power,
   No scholar can map them, no hunter can trap them,
   No man can deny: Die Gedanken sind frei.

2. So I think as I please, and this gives me pleasure,
   My conscience decrees this right I must treasure;
   My thoughts will not cater to duke or dictator;
   No man can deny: Die Gedanken sind frei!

3. And if tyrants take me and throw me in prison,
   My thoughts will burst free like blossoms in season.
   Foundations will crumble, the structure will tumble,
   And free men will cry: Die Gedanken sind frei!

1. Die Gedanken sind frei, wer kann sie erraten?
   Sie fliehen vorbei wie nachtliche Schatten.
   Kein Mensch kann sie wissen, kein Jäger erschiessen,
   Es bleibet dabei: Die Gedanken sind frei.

2. Ich denke was ich will, und was mich beglücket,
   Doch alles in der Still, und wie es sich schicket.
   Mein Wunsch und Begehren kann niemand verwehren;
   Es bleibet dabei: Die Gedanken sind frei.

3. Und sperrt man mich ein im finsteren Kerker,
   Das alles sind rein vergebliche Werke;
   Denn meine Gedanken zerreissen die Schranken
   Und Mauern entzwei: Die Gedanken sind frei.

This old German folk song is said to date back more than four hundred years. It apparently sprang from the Peasants' War of 1524-26, when the oppressed peasants revolted against increased exploitation by the nobles. Unfortunately, the peasants were routed by the princes and the Swabian League, and their defeat prolonged serfdom in Germany for nearly three centuries, stunting democratic development. However, this fine song continued to be sung whenever Germans made a new attempt to gain freedom. Schiller put it in one of his plays, and the German student movement took it up. It was widely sung in the schools of pre-Hitler Germany and German immigrants brought it with them when they came to this continent.

WHEN WILT THOU SAVE THE PEOPLE?

Music by JOSIAH BOOTH
Words by EBENEZER ELLIOTT

When wilt thou save the peo - ple? O, God of mer - cy, when? Not kings and lords, but na - tions! Not thrones and crowns, but men! Flow'rs of thy heart, O God, are they; Let them not pass like weeds a - way, Their he - ri - tage a sun - less day; God save the peo - ple!

1. When wilt thou save the people?
    O God of mercy, when?
Not kings and lords, but nations!
    Not thrones and crowns, but men!
Flowers of thy heart, O God, are they;
Let them not pass like weeds away,
Their heritage a sunless day;
    God save the people!

2. Shall crime bring crime for ever,
    Strength aiding still the strong?
Is it Thy will, O Father,
    That man shall toil for wrong?
"No," say Thy mountains; "No," Thy skies;
Man's clouded sun shall brightly rise,
And songs be heard instead of sighs:
    God save the people!

3. When wilt thou save the people?
    O God of mercy, when?
The people, Lord, the people,
    Not thrones and crowns, but men!
God save the people; Thine they are,
Thy children, as Thy angels fair;
From vice, oppression, and despair
    God save the people!

The words of this song were written by Ebenezer Elliott (1781-1849), a master-founder of Sheffield, England, who became famous in his day as the Corn-Law Rhymer. At the time "corn" meant wheat, and the corn laws imposed high duties on wheat imported into Britain, with the result that bread became very dear. In 1827, Elliott published a book called *Corn-Law Rhymes* in which he described the hardships imposed on the poor by the "bread-tax." A typical verse ran:

"I bought his coffin with my bed,
My gown bought earth and prayer;
I pawn'd my mother's ring for bread,
I pawn'd my father's chair."

The long struggle against the prohibitive duties was led by the Anti-Corn Law League headed by Richard Cobden and John Bright, and Sir Robert Peel finally abolished them in 1849, marking the beginning of England's free-trade policy.

"When Wilt Thou Save the People?" (which appeared in *Corn-Law Rhymes*) became the anthem of the Chartists, a reform movement active in Britain between 1838 and 1848. It was formed when some radical members of Parliament met with representatives of the Working-Men's Association and drew up a "People's Charter" demanding six reforms: universal suffrage, vote by ballot, equal electoral districts, payment of members of Parliament, abolition of the property qualification for members, and annual elections.

The Chartist Movement became quite powerful: monster meetings were held, several newspapers started, and gigantic petitions presented to Parliament. In 1848, the year of widespread revolution in Europe, the military, led by the Duke of Wellington, was called out to suppress Chartist demonstrations, and thereafter the movement died out. Although considered very radical in their day, all of the Chartists' demands except annual elections have since been achieved.

The song is now considered so respectable that it has found a place in the hymnals of several nations. Different tunes have been used for Elliott's words: one by Arthur Somervell is favored in England; the one given here, which is better known in the United States, is by Josiah Booth.

A NEW JERUSALEM

Words by WILLIAM BLAKE
Music by SIR C. HUBERT H. PARRY

Resolutely

And did those feet in an-cient time Walk u-pon Eng-land's moun-tains green? And was the Ho-ly Lamb of God On Eng-land's plea-sant pas-tures seen? And did the coun-te-nance di-vine shine forth u-pon our clou-ded hills? And was Je-ru-sa-lem buil-ded here a-mong these dark sa-ta-nic mills?

By permission of the executors of the late Sir Hubert Parry
and J. Curwen & Sons, Ltd., 24 Berners St., London W.1.

1. And did those feet in ancient time
   Walk upon England's mountains green?
   And was the Holy Lamb of God
   On England's pleasant pastures seen?

2. And did the countenance divine
   Shine forth upon our clouded hills?
   And was Jerusalem builded here
   Among these dark satanic mills?

3. Bring me my bow of burning gold!
   Bring me my arrows of desire!
   Bring me my spear! O clouds, unfold!
   Bring me my chariot of fire!

4. I will not cease from mental fight,
   Nor shall my sword sleep in my hand,
   Till we have built Jerusalem
   In England's green and pleasant land.

When the industrial revolution began to transform the traditional society of medieval England, it brought unbelievable suffering to the working people. The sturdy yeomen who had been the backbone of the nation were gradually squeezed out by enclosures of the common land and the development of farm machinery. Factories were springing up in the cities, and the farm laborers and hand craftsmen were being forced into the woolen and cotton mills of Yorkshire and Lancashire. Machinery meant long hours and few jobs, and wages were so low that parents had to send their children to work as soon as they could hold a broom. Steam created a heavy demand for coal, and by the beginning of the nineteenth century much of England's once-green landscape was bare and black.

The rural customs that had given color and zest to the working man's life disappeared as the "jolly ploughboys" and independent hand-weavers were forced into the long, dark factories. Bewildered and downcast by their new life, they had no heart to sing, but one of England's great poets gave voice to their unexpressed feelings of revolt in these noble verses.

William Blake (1757-1827) was a remarkable man: a versatile artist who not only wrote some of England's finest poetry but also illustrated and engraved a whole series of books. He was a mystic, but he never lost touch with reality, and he was profoundly shocked by the suffering he saw around him. His indictment of England's "dark Satanic mills" and his challenge to build "The New Jerusalem" here on earth appeared in 1804. The verses were later set to music by the English composer, Sir Hubert Parry (1848-1918).

LA MARSEILLAISE

Words and music by ROUGET DE LISLE
Translation by CHARLES H. KERR

(over)

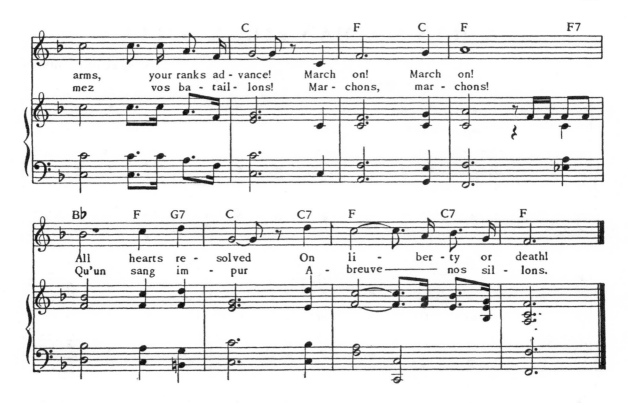

The French national anthem is not only the most stirring of all national anthems: it is practically *the* international song of revolt. Yet, strangely enough, the song was not conceived as an expression of rebellion. Its composer, Claude Joseph Rouget de Lisle (1760-1836), was a young French captain who was completely loyal to his king.

In April, 1792, when Rouget de Lisle was stationed at Strasbourg, news came that France had declared war on Prussia and Hungary, and the young officer, who was known to be a talented musician, was urged to write a patriotic song. He immediately wrote the "Chant de guerre pour l'armée du Rhin," dedicating it to Marshal Lukner, Commander-in-Chief of the Army of the Rhine.

The song was published both in Strasbourg and in Paris, and at once became very popular. In June, it was sung at a banquet in Marseilles, just as a battalion of volunteers was leaving for Paris. They sang it all along their route, and on August 10, when they joined the storming of the Tuileries, they roared it out with such enthusiasm that it was immediately taken up by the frenzied Paris mob. It was from these Marseilles volunteers that the song got its name of the "Marseillaise."

The tyrants against whom Rouget de Lisle had directed his fiery song were German princes, and the howling hordes of slaves he had in mind were Prussian soldiers, but the sense was quickly interpreted in the light of the revolutionary situation. Contemporary accounts describe the powerful impression the song made wherever and whenever it was heard.

By an ironic turn, its creator almost lost his head to the revolutionary forces who had taken over his song. Because of his royalist sympathies he was discharged from the army and imprisoned, but he escaped the guillotine and in 1794 he re-enlisted in the army of the French Republic.

On July 15, 1795, the Marseillaise was declared the official national anthem of France. It became a symbol of the Revolution: of the "Rights of Man," of "Liberty, Equality, and Fraternity," and as such was taken up by revolutionary movements in other European countries. In 1830, it again proved its power to inspire the masses: it was sung in the July Revolution by the radical workers of Paris when they overthrew the reactionary King Charles X and put Louis Philippe on the throne. Subsequently, Louis granted Rouget de Lisle a pension, and when he died in 1836, huge crowds of industrial workers walked bare-headed in his funeral procession.

A MAN'S A MAN FOR A' THAT

Words by ROBERT BURNS

rank is but the gui-nea's stamp; The man's the gowd for a' that.

1. Is there, for honest poverty,
   That hangs his head, and a' that?
   The coward slave, we pass him by,
   We dare be poor for a' that!
     For a' that, and a' that,
     Our toils obscure and a' that;
     The rank is but the guinea's stamp;
     The man's the gowd for a' that.

2. What though on hamely fare we dine,
   Wear hodden-gray, and a' that?
   Gie fools their silks, and knaves their wine,
   A man's a man for a' that.
     For a' that, and a' that,
     Their tinsel show, and a' that;
     The honest man, though e'er sae poor,
     Is king o' men for a' that.

3. Ye see yon birkie ca'd a lord,
   Wha struts, and stares, and a' that;
   Though hundreds worship at his word,
   He's but a coof for a' that.
     For a' that, and a' that,
     His riband, star, and a' that,
     The man o' independent mind,
     He looks and laughs at a' that.

4. A prince can mak' a belted knight,
   A marquis, duke, and a' that;
   But an honest man's aboon his might,
   Guid faith, he mauna fa' that!
     For a' that, and a' that,
     Their dignities, and a' that,
     The pith o' sense, and pride o' worth,
     Are higher rank than a' that.

5. Then let us pray that come it may,
   As come it will for a' that,
   That sense and worth, o'er a' the earth,
   May bear the gree, and a' that.
     For a' that, and a' that,
     It's coming yet, for a' that,
     That man to man the world o'er
     Shall brothers be for a' that.

Robert Burns (1759–1796), Scotland's favorite bard, rejoiced in his title of "the ploughman poet," and many of his verses celebrate the dignity of honest labor.

Burns always cherished his own independence and his right to meet any man on equal terms. Sir Walter Scott remarked of him: "Although so poor as to be ever on the brink of ruin, he was as proud and independent as if he possessed a prince's revenue," and Burns himself wrote: "Amid my poverty I am as independent and more happy than a monarch of the world. I can look on a worthless fellow of a duke with unqualified contempt, and can regard an honest scavenger with sincere respect."

"A Man's A Man for A' That" is probably the best expression of Burns' social and political philosophy. His life spanned two great democratic revolutions: the American and the French, and in this song, written in 1795, just a year before his death, he gave poetic form to the ideas that inspired them. One critic has described it as a rhymed version of Tom Paine's *The Rights of Man*.

188

JEFFERSON AND LIBERTY

1. The gloomy night before us flies,
   The reign of terror now is o'er;
   Its gags, inquisitors, and spies,
   Its herds of harpies are no more!

CHORUS:
   Rejoice, Columbia's sons, rejoice!
   To tyrants never bend the knee,
   But join with heart, and soul, and voice,
   For Jefferson and liberty!

2. No lordling here, with gorging jaws
   Shall wring from industry the food;
   Nor fiery bigot's holy laws
   Lay waste our fields and streets in blood!

3. Here strangers from a thousand shores
   Compelled by tyranny to roam,
   Shall find, amidst abundant stores,
   A nobler and happier home.

4. Here Art shall lift her laurelled head,
   Wealth, Industry, and Peace, divine;
   And where dark, pathless forests spread,
   Rich fields and lofty cities shine.

5. From Europe's wants and woes remote,
   A friendly waste of waves between,
   Here plenty cheers the humblest cot,
   And smiles on every village green.

6. Here free as air, expanded space,
   To every soul and sect shall be—
   That sacred privilege of our race—
   The worship of the Deity.

7. Let foes to freedom dread the name;
   But should they touch the sacred tree,
   Twice fifty thousand swords would flame
   For Jefferson and liberty.

8. From Georgia to Lake Champlain,
   From seas to Mississippi's shore,
   Ye sons of freedom loud proclaim—
   "The reign of terror is no more."

From 1796 to 1800, when John Adams was President, the United States government was dominated by the Federalists, the party of rank and privilege. The immigrants, who were coming to America to escape poverty and oppression in their native lands, naturally aligned themselves with the new Democratic-Republican Party.

In 1798, when there was danger of the country being drawn into war with France, the Federalists took advantage of the crisis to pass the "Alien and Sedition Acts" to suppress their political opponents. These acts empowered the President to expel "dangerous aliens," provided for indictment of those who should "unlawfully combine or conspire" against the administration or should write or speak "with intent to defame" the government. Twenty-five newspapermen were prosecuted and ten were convicted under the Sedition Act — all of them members of the Democratic-Republican Party.

Feelings ran high in the election of 1800 in which Thomas Jefferson became President. Jefferson was pledged to repeal the oppressive laws, and the people acclaimed him their champion in this rousing song. It is interesting to note that the English people had sung "Wilkes and Liberty" back in 1769 when John Wilkes was expelled from Parliament for daring to criticize a royal edict, and "Lincoln and Liberty" was destined to be the most famous song of the 1860 campaign.

THE RED FLAG

Words by JIM CONNELL

1. The people's flag is deepest red,
   It shrouded oft our martyred dead,
   And ere their limbs grew stiff and cold
   Their hearts' blood dyed its ev'ry fold.

CHORUS: Then raise the scarlet standard high!
   Within its shade we'll live or die.
   Though cowards flinch and traitors sneer,
   We'll keep the red flag flying here.

2. It waved above our infant might
   When all ahead seemed dark as night;
   It witnessed many a deed and vow:
   We must not change its color now.

3. It well recalls the triumphs past;
   It gives the hope of peace at last—
   The banner bright, the symbol plain
   Of human right and human gain.

4. With heads uncovered swear we all
   To bear it onward till we fall.
   Come dungeon dark or gallows grim,
   This song shall be our parting hymn.

To most Americans the symbol of the red flag is associated exclusively with the Communist Party. But years before the Communists took it over it had been the banner of the working classes and democratic socialists of Europe and also of the socialist parties on this continent.

The song, "The Red Flag," is the official anthem of the British Labour Party. It used to be sung by the Wobblies in the United States and Canada, although it is rarely heard now on this side of the Atlantic.

The words were written in 1889 by Jim Connell, an Irish journalist who used to say: "I was educated under a hedge for a few weeks." Connell was inspired to write his most famous song by the great London dock strike in 1889. He sent it to a weekly paper called *Justice*; it appeared in the Christmas issue, and within a week it was being sung in Liverpool and Glasgow. It has continued to be popular in England right down to the present.

Jim Connell originally set his words to the tune of "The White Cockade," an old Jacobite song. Later Adolphe Smith Headingley started the custom of singing it to the tune of "Maryland" (or "Tannenbaum"), and that is the tune used today.

On August 1, 1945, "The Red Flag" was sung in the British House of Commons. Parliament had just assembled after the election in which Labour had defeated the Conservative government of Sir Winston Churchill. This account of the incident was given in *The Daily Herald*, a British labor newspaper.

"George Lansbury (a famous Labour M.P.) may have passed on, but he was responsible yesterday for the singing of 'The Red Flag' in the Commons. W. H. Guy, the M.P. who succeeds to George's seat, could not resist it. When the Tories, seeing Winston enter the House, greeted him with 'For He's a Jolly Good Fellow,' Guy said to Jim Griffiths (a miner M.P.): 'We can't let them get away with that! If you start "The Red Flag," I'll conduct it.' So he waved his arms while Griffiths . . . started 'The people's flag is deepest red,' and his Labour colleagues stood up and joined him.

"It was T. G. Thomas, the young schoolmaster who won Cardiff Central (a Welsh riding) who spoke to me of the emotion he felt while he sang the Socialist Anthem which had heartened so many in the dark days, and which he had learned from the pioneers in his childhood. 'How they sang it in the Rhondda after the election!' he said. 'How the crowds cheered and how the old people wept with joy! I little dreamed I should live to be an M.P. on a day like this!' "

THE PEATBOG SOLDIERS

With determination

Far and wide as the eye can wan-der, Heath and bog are ev'-ry-

where. Not a bird sings out to cheer us, Oaks are stand-ing,

gaunt and bare. We are the peat-bog sol-diers; we're march-ing

rit - - - - -   *a tempo*

with our spades to the bog.   We bog.

1. Far and wide as the eye can wander,
   Heath and bog are ev'rywhere.
   Not a bird sings out to cheer us,
   Oaks are standing, gaunt and bare.

CHORUS: We are the peat-bog soldiers,
   We're marching with our spades
   To the bog. (Repeat)

2. Up and down the guards are pacing,
   No one, no one can go through;
   Flight would mean a sure death facing,
   Guns and barbed wire greet our view.

3. But for us there is no complaining,
   Winter will in time be past;
   One day we shall cry rejoicing:
   "Homeland dear, you're mine at last!"

LAST CHORUS:
   Then will the peat-bog soldiers
   March no more with their spades
   To the bog.

1. Wohin auch das Auge blicket,
   Moor und Heide nur ringsheram.
   Vogelsang uns nicht erquicket,
   Eichen stehen kahl und krumm.

CHORUS: Wir sin die Moorsoldaten
   Und ziehen mit dem Spaten
   Ins Moor. (Repeat)

2. Auf und nieder geh'n die Posten,
   Keiner, keiner kann hindurch.
   Flucht wird nur das Leben kosten!
   Vierfach ist umzäunt die Burg.

3. Doch für uns gibt es kein Klagen,
   Ewig kann's nicht Winter sein.
   Einmal werden froh wir sagen:
   "Heimat, du bist wieder mein."

LAST CHORUS:
   Dann zieh'n die Moorsoldaten,
   Nicht mehr mit dem Spaten
   Ins Moor.

After the American Civil War the traditional type of slavery largely disappeared from the world, but in the twentieth century another form of slavery developed: a slavery whose symbol was not the auction block but the concentration camp, that favorite weapon of the totalitarian state. The world first became aware of this new threat to freedom in Hitler's Germany when socialists and intellectuals and labor leaders and Jews were thrown behind barbed wire. The men in the concentration camps had no weapons to fight, but their will to resist remained. That unbroken resistance found expression in the famous "Moorsoldaten." Day after day the prisoners were marched to the bog to dig peat, and as they marched with their spades over their shoulders they sang this song of "The Peatbog Soldiers." It is still an unexplained mystery why the guards allowed it: certainly the meaning of the last verse could hardly be missed. It has been reported that prisoners sang it with such gusto that the song was finally forbidden.

Actual details of the origin of the song are sparse. It is generally believed that it originated in the Borgermoor concentration camp in 1933, but the *Fireside Book of Folk Songs* notes that Pierre Martinot, the designer of that book, who was a prisoner in Dachau in 1944-45, says that the old prisoners there claimed the song was created in Dachau and carried by underground to Borgermoor. During the Spanish Civil War it was a favorite marching song of the International Brigade. It was notated by Hanns Eisler, and his version has become known in many countries.

KEVIN BARRY

1. Early on a Monday morning,
   High upon the gallows tree
   Kevin Barry gave his young life
   For the cause of liberty.
   Just a lad of eighteen summers,
   Yet there's no one can deny
   As he went to death that morning
   Proudly held his head up high.

2. "Shoot me like an Irish soldier;
   Do not hang me like a dog;
   For I fought for Ireland's freedom
   On that cold September morn—
   All around that little bakery
   Where we fought them hand to hand.
   Shoot me like an Irish soldier
   For I fought to free Ireland."

3. Another martyr for old Ireland,
Another murder for the crown!
Brutal laws to crush the Irish
Could not keep their spirit down.
Lads like Barry are no cowards:
From their foes they do not fly,
For their bravery always has been
Ireland's cause to live or die.

4. Just before he faced the hangman
In his lonely prison cell,
British soldiers tortured Barry
Just because he would not tell
All the names of his companions,
Other things they wished to know;
"Turn informer and we'll free you."
Proudly Barry answered, "No."

The dominating feature of Ireland's history for nearly a thousand years was her struggle to throw off the yoke of English domination, and from that struggle sprang scores of revolutionary ballads. Perhaps the most popular of these is "Kevin Barry," which commemorates one of the last patriots to die for Ireland's freedom.

By 1914 the British Government had finally agreed to grant Home Rule to Ireland, but when war broke out it was again postponed. Embittered by the many delays, the Irish nationalists attempted to establish a republic through the Easter Rebellion of 1916. This failed, but in 1920 the Republic was again proclaimed in Dublin. In a final effort to suppress it, the English Government sent in the troops who soon became infamous as "the Black and Tans." Finally, in 1921, Britain recognized De Valera's Free State, and Ireland's long martyrdom came to an end.

But before that day arrived, young Kevin Barry, an eighteen-year-old student who had enlisted in the Republican Army, was captured in an ambush in which a British soldier was killed. He was hanged in the Dublin jail on November 1, 1920, but this song has kept his memory green wherever Irishmen are found. Ironically enough, its rebellious lines are set to the tune of an old British sea song, "Rolling Home to Dear Old England." The second stanza is sometimes repeated as a chorus.

LET US ALL SPEAK OUR MINDS

Music by J. G. MAEDER
Words by WILLIAM BROUGH

(over)

2. For we know it's all fudge to say man's the best judge
   Of what should be and shouldn't, and so on,
   That woman should bow, nor attempt to say how
   She considers that matters should go on.
   I never yet gave up myself thus a slave,
   However my husband might try for it;
   For I can't and I won't, and I shan't and I don't,
   But I will speak my mind if I die for it!

3. And all ladies I hope who've with husbands to cope,
   With the rights of the sex will not trifle.
   We all, if we choose, our tongues but to use
   Can all opposition soon stifle.
   Let man, if he will, then bid us be still
   And silent, a price he'll pay high for it,
   For we won't and we can't and we don't and we shan't,
   Let us all speak our minds if we die for it!

By the end of the nineteenth century the philosophy of "A Man's a Man for A' That" was fairly widely accepted in Britain and America, but though people might argue that all men should have equal rights, few could imagine such a principle being extended to women.

As wives and mothers, women have traditionally been subordinate to their husbands, and their struggle to win their independence lasted longer and aroused almost as bitter feeling as the anti-slavery movement. In 1848 Lucretia Mott and Elizabeth Cady Stanton called the first American Rights Convention in Seneca Falls, New York, and soon women's rights groups in many parts of the country were holding local conventions and pressing for women's suffrage.

As most suffragettes were active Abolitionists, they were swept up in the anti-slavery battle, and it was not until after the Civil War that the rights of women to vote became a burning issue. By heckling at political rallies, holding spectacular parades, printing thousands of posters and pamphlets, and singing lively propaganda songs, the suffragettes tried to convince men that they were people, too. Ignoring the jeers of rude men and the social disapproval of more conventional women, they kept hammering away at their thesis until at last they began to win a few male legislators to their cause.

The first victory came in 1869 when the Territory of Wyoming adopted a constitution guaranteeing "equal political rights for all male and female citizens": a clause that gave Wyoming its nickname of "The Equality State." By 1912 votes for women had become a major national issue, and finally in 1920 the Congress passed the Nineteenth Amendment to the Constitution providing that "The right of the citizens of the United States to vote shall not be denied or abridged by the United States or by any state on account of sex."

Like the trade unionists, the suffragettes recognized the value of singing for stirring up enthusiasm. Between the Civil War and 1920 they composed and sang many verses, setting them largely to well known tunes like "Hold the Fort," "The Bonnie Blue Flag," "Auld Lang Syne," or the ubiquitous "John Brown's Body."

Today most of the suffragette verses sound unbearably sentimental or heavily pedantic, but they did manage to get their points across. Like modern advertisers, they could exploit the emotional appeal of the word "mother" in "Giving the Ballot to the Mothers," or express their anti-liquor bias in the promise that "Women's vote will save the home." They could describe women's contribution to society:

"Women have reared all the sons of the brave,
Women have shared in the burdens they gave,
Women have labored *your* country to save,
That's why we're wanting to vote!"

or appeal to history and logic:

"To tax one who's not represented
Is tyranny — tell if you can
Why women should not have the ballot?
She's taxed just the same as a man."

One of the best songs to come out of women's struggle for freedom was "Let Us All Speak Our Minds," which puts the feminist case quite emphatically but still manages to temper it with a little humor. In *Songs of Yesterday* Philip D. Jordan noted:

"The songs of women's independence were both applauded and hissed during America's coming of age, but none received more defiant approval or contempt than the song of the militant feminist, 'Let Us All Speak Our Minds If We Die For It.'"

IT COULD BE A WONDERFUL WORLD

Music by LOU SINGER
Words by HY ZARET

In 1947, Hy Zaret and Lou Singer wrote their now-famous "Little Songs on Big Subjects." Originally commissioned as Public Service "spot announcements" for radio station WNEW in New York City, the songs were recorded by "The Jesters" and immediately caught listeners' fancy. The Institute of Democratic Education then made the records available to other radio stations, and within a few months they had played over five hundred stations throughout the country.

Since then, these "Mother Goose Songs of Democracy" have been heard on the air more than a hundred thousand times; have been praised by leading educators across the country, and have won a variety of awards and citations. William Rose Benet commented that "'Little Songs on Big Subjects' is the Bill of Rights set to music." The best of the group, "It Could Be A Wonderful World," effectively promotes the idea that all men are brothers.

EVERYBODY LOVES SATURDAY NIGHT

1. Bobo waro fero Satodeh,
   Bobo waro, bobo waro,
   Bobo waro, bobo waro,
   Bobo waro fero Satodeh.

2. Everybody loves Saturday night,
   Everybody, everybody,
   Everybody, everybody,
   Everybody loves Saturday night.

3. Tout le monde aime Samedi soir.
   Tout le monde, tout le monde,
   Tout le monde, tout le monde,
   Tout le monde aime Samedi soir.
   (French)

4. Jeder eyne hot lieb Shabas ba nacht,
   Jeder eyne hot, jeder eyne hot,
   Jeder eyne hot, jeder eyne hot,
   Jeder eyne hot lieb Shabas ba nacht.
   (Yiddish)

5. A todos les gusta la noche del Sabado,
   A todos les, a todos les,
   A todos les, a todos les,
   A todos les gusta la noche del Sabado.
   (Spanish)

6. Ren ren si huan li pai lu,
   Ren ren si huan, ren ren si huan,
   Ren ren si huan, ren ren si huan,
   Ren ren si huan li pai lu.
   (Chinese)

7. Vsiem nravitsa sabbota vietcheram,
   Vsiem nravitsa, vsiem nravitsa,
   Vsiem nravitsa, vsiem nravitsa,
   Vsiem nravitsa sabbota vietcheram.
   (Russian)

This gay little song is said to have originated in the West African colony of Nigeria at a time when the British authorities had imposed an evening curfew and the Nigerians had succeeded in getting it lifted on Saturday nights. Every week they held outdoor festivals at which they sang this as a means of expressing their defiance. Later, it spread to other countries, and when Peter Seeger heard it in Los Angeles in 1951, he started the custom of translating its one-line lyric into many languages.

HEY, HO, NOBODY HOME

GOING TO STUDY WAR NO MORE

2. Goin' to put on my long white robe
Down by the riverside, down by the riverside, down by the riverside,
Goin' to put on my long white robe
Down by the riverside, and study war no more.

3. Goin' to talk with the Prince of Peace
Down by the riverside, down by the riverside, down by the riverside,
Goin' to talk with the Prince of Peace
Down by the riverside, and study war no more.

Thousands of years ago an Old Testament prophet wrote that when the Lord's kingdom was established, "They shall beat their swords into plowshares, and their spears into pruning-hooks; nation shall not lift up sword against nation, neither shall they learn war any more. But they shall sit every man under his vine and under his fig tree; and none shall make them afraid." (Micah 4, 3-4). This great Negro spiritual expresses the age-old longing for peace in simple and irresistible terms.

RECORD LIST

This is not intended as a complete discography of industrial or trade-union songs, but merely as a guide to recorded versions of the particular songs included in this volume.

The list gives the more important albums or long-playing records of labor songs, indicating which of the songs in this book are found on each. Some other records of a more general nature have been added where they contain one or more "Songs of Work and Freedom" not otherwise covered. The object is to give at least one recorded version of each song, except for a few which are very well known, and a few others which have not been recorded. Although some songs may be found on several records, no attempt has been made to give all the records of any particular song.

Most of the records are long-playing, and are currently available, although a few important out-of-print items have also been listed.

ALMANAC SINGERS: *The Original "Talking Union" with the Almanac Singers and Other Union Songs with Peter Seeger and Chorus.* Folkways FH 5285. "We Shall Not Be Moved," "Roll the Union On," "Casey Jones," "Miner's Lifeguard," "Solidarity Forever," "You Gotta Go Down and Join the Union," "Hold the Fort," "Get Thee Behind Me, Satan," "Union Maid," "All I Want," "Talking Union," "Union Train," "Which Side Are You On?"

JOE GLAZER: *Songs of Work and Freedom.* Washington Records WR-460. "Solidarity Forever," "Talking Union," "West Virginia Hills," "Union Man," "My Sweetheart's the Mule in the Mines," "Dark as a Dungeon," "Hard Times in the Mill," "The Mill Was Made of Marble," "The Farmer Is the Man," "Planting Rice," "Automation," "The Man That Waters the Workers' Beer," "It Could Be a Wonderful World," "Kevin Barry."

JOE GLAZER: *The Songs of Joe Hill.* Folkways FA 2039. "Casey Jones," "Joe Hill," "The Preacher and the Slave."

JOE GLAZER AND BILL FRIEDLAND: *Songs of the Wobblies,* Labor Arts 3. "Hallelujah, I'm a Bum!" "The Commonwealth of Toil," "The Preacher and the Slave," "Down to the Soupline," "The Popular Wobbly."

JOE GLAZER AND THE ELM CITY FOUR: *Eight New Songs for Labor.* CIO Department of Education and Research. "Great Day," "Too Old to Work," "We Will Overcome," "The Mill Was Made of Marble." (78 RPM)

JOE GLAZER: *"The Song of the Guaranteed Wage,"* UAW-CIO Education Dept. (45 RPM).

TOM GLAZER: *Favorite American Union Songs,* CIO Department of Education and Research. "Solidarity Forever," "We Shall Not Be Moved," "Casey Jones," "Which Side Are You On?", "Union Maid," "On the Picket Line," "Going Down the Road," "We Are Building a Strong Union." "Roll the Union On." (78 RPM)

JOHN GREENWAY: *American Industrial Folksongs.* Riverside 12-607. "Hard Times in the Mill," "Dark as a Dungeon," "Too Old to Work," "Mother Jones," "Down on Roberts' Farm" (Down on Penny's Farm).

   "The Great American Bum," Riverside 12-619. "Going Down the Road," "Hard Travelin'," "Acres of Clams," "Hallelujah, I'm a Bum."

WOODY GUTHRIE: *"Talking Dust Bowl."* Folkways FA 2011. "So Long It's Been Good to Know You," "Blowing Down This Road Feeling Bad."

HOOTENANNY TONIGHT! Folkways FN 2511. "The Rich Man and the Poor Man," "Talking Union," "Dark as a Dungeon."

THE JESTERS: *Little Songs on Big Subjects.* Public Service Records. "It Could Be a Wonderful World."

ELIZABETH KNIGHT: *Songs of the Suffragettes.* Folkways FH 5281. "Let Us All Speak Our Minds."

TONY KRABER: *"The Old Chisholm Trail."* Mercury MG 20008. "The Old Chisholm Trail."

LEADBELLY: *"Take This Hammer."* Folkways FA 2004. "Take This Hammer."

LIBRARY OF CONGRESS: *Songs and Ballads of the Anthracite Miners.* AAFS L.16. "Union Man," "Down in a Coal Mine."

HARRY McCLINTOCK: *"This Land Is My Land."* Folkways FC 7027. "Jerry, Go and Oil That Car."

EWAN MACCOLL: *"Fourpence a Day"* and other British Industrial Folk Songs. Stinson SLP 79. "Poor Paddy Works on the Railway," "The Blantyre Explosion," "Fourpence a Day."

ALAN MILLS: *Songs of the Sea.* Folkways FA 2312. "New Bedford Whalers" (Blow Ye Winds in the Morning); "Leave Her, Johnny."

HERMES NYE: *Ballads of the Civil War.* Folkways FA 2187. "Abolitionist Hymn," "John Brown's Body," "Battle Hymn of the Republic."

ODETTA: *Odetta Sings Ballads and Blues.* Tradition TLP 1010. "O Freedom."

GENE AND FRANCESCA RASKIN: *We Work and Sing.* International Ladies' Garment Workers' Union. "ILGWU Anthem," "Bread and Roses," "We Are Building a Strong Union," "We Shall Not Be Moved," "Are You Sleeping?", "Hold the Fort," "Solidarity Forever."

WALT ROBERTSON: *American Northwest Ballads.* Folkways FA 2046. "Life Is a Toil," "Acres of Clams."

PAUL ROBESON: *Robeson.* Vanguard VRS 9037. "Jerusalem," "John Brown's Body."
  Let Freedom Sing! Othello L-301. "Kevin Barry," "John Brown's Body," "Joe Hill."
  "Swing Low, Sweet Chariot." Columbia ML 2038. "No More Auction Block."

EARL ROBINSON: *Americana.* Mercury MG 20008. "Jefferson and Liberty," "Drill, Ye Tarriers, Drill."

PETER SEEGER: *Frontier Ballads, Vol. 1.* Folkways FA 2175. "No Irish Need Apply."
  Frontier Ballads, Vol. 2. Folkways FA 2176. "Paddy Works on the Railway," "My Sweetheart's the Mule in the Mine."
  "Darling Corey." Folkways FA 2003. "Down on Penny's Farm."
  American Industrial Ballads. Folkways FH 5251. "The Buffalo Skinners," "The Farmer Is the Man," "Beans, Bacon and Gravy," "Winnsboro Cotton Mill Blues," "Eight Hours," "Hard Times in the Mill," "Seven Cent Cotton."
  A Pete Seeger Concert. Stinson SLP 57. "Winnsboro Cotton Mill Blues," "Paddy Works on the Railroad," "Die Gedanken Sind Frei."
  "The Pete Seeger Sampler." Folkways FA 2043. "Lullaby" (Times Is Mighty Hard), "Depression Blues" (Beans, Bacon, and Gravy).
  Gazette. Folkways FN 2501. "Forty-Two Kids" (Teacher's Lament).
  Folk Songs for Young People. Folkways FA 7532. "The Farmer Is the Man," "The Washer Lad," "John Henry," "It Could Be a Wonderful World," "So Long, It's Been Good to Know You."

MERLE TRAVIS: *Back Home.* Capitol T 891. "Sixteen Tons," "Dark as a Dungeon," "John Henry."

SONGS OF THE INTERNATIONAL BRIGADE. Stinson SLP 25. "Die Moorsoldaten" (The Peat-Bog Soldiers).

THE WEAVERS: *The Weavers on Tour.* Vanguard VRS 9013. "Drill Ye Tarriers," "Fi-li-mi-oo-re-ay" (Pat Works on the Railway), "The Boll Weevil," "So Long It's Been Good to Know You."

READING LIST

The list below is far from an exhaustive bibliography either of labor songs or of labor history, but it does include most of the books, pamphlets, and periodicals which the authors consulted in preparing this volume. It should be useful for anyone who wants more information on any of the people, movements, or events mentioned in the notes.

AFL-CIO Songbook: AFL-CIO Dept. of Education, Washington, 1958.

Russell Ames: *The Story of American Folk Song.* Grosset & Dunlap, New York, 1955.

Saul Alinsky: *John L. Lewis.* C. P. Putnam's Sons, New York, 1949.

William Rose Benet and Norman Cousins: *The Poetry of Freedom.* Modern Library, New York, 1948.

Ralph Chaplin: *Wobbly.* University of Chicago Press, Chicago, 1948.

Louis Chappell: *John Henry, A Folklore Study.* Jena: Frommansche Verlag, Walter Biedermann, 1933.

John R. Commons: *History of Labor in the United States.* Vols. I and II, 1918; Vols. III and IV, 1935.

Foster Rhea Dulles: *Labor in America.* Thomas Y. Crowell Co., New York, 1949.

Everybody Sings: Education Department, International Ladies' Garment Workers' Union, New York, 1956.

John Greenway: *American Folk Songs of Protest.* University of Pennsylvania Press, Philadelphia, 1953.

Woody Guthrie: *Bound for Glory.* E. P. Dutton, New York, 1943.

William D. Haywood: *Bill Haywood's Book.* International Publishers, New York, 1929.

Waldemar Hille: *The People's Song Book.* Boni and Gaer, New York, 1948. (Reprint, 1956.)

Highlander Song Book (mimeographed): Highlander Folk School, c. 1945.

IWW Songs. Songs of the Workers (*To Fan the Flames of Discontent*), IWW Publishing Co., Chicago. 29th edition, 1956.

The Autobiography of Mother Jones. Charles H. Kerr, Chicago, 1925.

Jordan, Philip D. & Lillian Kessler: *Songs of Yesterday.* Doubleday, Doran, Garden City, 1941.

George Korson: *Minstrels of the Mine Patch.* University of Pennsylvania Press, Philadelphia, 1938.
    Coal Dust on the Fiddle. University of Pennsylvania Press, Philadelphia, 1943.
    Pennsylvania Songs and Legends. University of Pennsylvania Press, Philadelphia, 1949.

Labour Party Song Book. British Labour Party, London, 1955.

Labor Scrapbook. Education Department, United Rubber Workers, Akron, 1956.

A. L. Lloyd: *The Singing Englishman.* Workers' Music Association, London, 1951.
    Come All Ye Bold Miners. Lawrence and Wishart, London, 1952.
    Coal-Dust Ballads. Workers' Music Association, London, 1952.

John A. and Alan Lomax: *American Ballads and Folk Songs.* Macmillan, New York, 1934.
    Our Singing Country. Macmillan, New York, 1941.
    Folk Song, U.S.A. Duall, Sloan & Pierce, New York, 1947.

Ewan MacColl: *The Shuttle and the Cage.* Hargail Music Press, New York, 1954.

George Milburn: *The Hobo's Hornbook.* Ives, Washburn, New York, 1930.

Reginald Nettel: *Sing a Song of England.* Phoenix, London, 1954.

People's Songs. Periodical. People's Songs, Inc., New York. Feb. 1946 - Feb. 1949.

Rebel Song Book. Rand School Press, New York, c. 1935.

Carl Sandburg: *The American Songbag.* Harcourt, Brace, New York, 1927.

Elie Siegmeister and Olin Downes: *A Treasury of American Song.* Knopf, New York, 1943.

Irwin Silber: *Lift Every Voice.* People's Artists, New York, 1955.

Sing Out: Periodical. People's Artists, Inc., New York, May, 1950-

Singing Farmers. National Farmers' Union, Denver, 1947.

Song Book. National Rural Electrical Cooperative Association, Washington, 1953.

Barrie Stavis: *The Man Who Never Died.* Haven Press, New York, 1954.

Barrie Stavis and Frank Harmon: *Songs of Joe Hill,* People's Artists, New York, 1955.

Wallace Stegner: *The Preacher and the Slave.* Houghton, Boston, 1950.

Fred Thompson: *The IWW: Its First Fifty Years.* Industrial Workers of the World, Chicago, 1955.

Tom Tippett: *When Southern Labor Stirs.* Jonathan Cape and Harrison Smith, New York, 1931.

UAW-CIO Sings. UAW-CIO Education Department, Detroit, 1943.

Workers' Songs. Brookwood Labor College, Katonah, New York, c. 1934.

INDEX OF TITLES AND FIRST LINES

A miner's life is like a sailor's.................. 65
ABOLITIONIST HYMN, THE................167
ACRES OF CLAMS..........................138
Allons, enfants de la patrie......................183
And did those feet in ancient time...............182
ANTHEM OF THE ILGWU, THE.............. 78
Are you sleeping?............................ 29
As we come marching......................... 70
AUTOMATION 146
Aye ban a farmer in Minnesota..................110

BATTLE HYMN OF THE REPUBLIC, THE......172
BEANS, BACON, AND GRAVY................132
BLANTYRE EXPLOSION, THE................ 60
BLOW YE WINDS IN THE MORNING.........112
Bobo waro fero Satodeh.........................200
BOLL WEEVIL, THE........................... 98
BREAD AND ROSES........................... 70
BROTHER JOHN.............................. 29
BUFFALO SKINNERS, THE....................120
By Clyde's bonny banks where I sadly did
    wander 60

CANADAY-I-O 118
CASEY JONES 43
Come all of you good workers................... 54
Come all ye jolly fellows........................118
Come all ye railroad section men................ 88
Come all you young fellows..................... 49
Come along boys and listen to my tale............122
Come you ladies and you gentlemen..............100
COMMONWEALTH OF TOIL, THE.............. 14
CUTTY WREN, THE...........................175

DARK AS A DUNGEON........................ 49
DEATH OF MOTHER JONES, THE............. 58
DIE GEDANKEN SIND FREI...................178
Die Gedanken sind frei, my thoughts freely flower..178
DODGER, THE................................150

DOWN IN A COAL MINE...................... 47
DOWN ON PENNY'S FARM....................100
DRILL YE TARRIERS, DRILL................. 86

Early on a Monday morning....................194
EIGHT HOUR DAY, THE....................... 26
ELEVEN CENT COTTON.......................104
Every morning at half-past four.................. 68
Every morning at seven o'clock.................. 86
EVERYBODY LOVES SATURDAY NIGHT.......200

Far and wide as the eye can wander.............192
FARMER IS THE MAN, THE................... 96
FOURPENCE A DAY..........................134

GET THEE BEHIND ME, SATAN............... 28
GO DOWN, MOSES...........................168
GOING DOWN THE ROAD FEELING BAD......128
GOING TO STUDY WAR NO MORE...........202
Going to put on my long white robe..............202
GREAT DAY................................. 40

HALLELUJAH, I'M A BUM.....................126
HARD TIMES IN THE MILL................... 68
HARD TRAVELING...........................124
HEY HO, NOBODY HOME.....................201
Hey ho, nobody home.........................201
HINKY DINKY PARLEZ-VOUS................. 31
HOLD THE FORT............................ 36

I am a jovial collier lad........................... 47
I been having some hard traveling................124
I DON'T WANT YOUR MILLIONS, MISTER......160
I don't want your millions, Mister................160
I dreamed I saw Joe Hill last night.............. 20
I dreamed that I had died....................... 76
I think I sing this little song..................... 62
I thought I heard the old man say................114
I was born long ago in eighteen ninety-one.........132
I was standing 'round a defense town one day..... 90

I went down, down, down to the factory............146
If each little kid could have fresh milk each day....198
If the boss is in the way, we're gonna roll it over him 44
If you want higher wages, let me tell you what to do. 22
I'll tell you the story of Jonathan Tweed..........162
I'm a decent boy just landed from the town
    of Ballyfadd....................................152
I'm goin' down the road feelin' bad................128
In eighteen hundred and forty-one................. 84
In the gloom of mighty cities..................... 14
Is there for honest poverty.......................186
IT COULD BE A WONDERFUL WORLD........198
I've got a mule and her name is Sal...............115
I've sung this song but I'll sing it again..........107
I've wandered all over this country...............138

JEFFERSON AND LIBERTY....................188
JERRY, GO AND OIL THAT CAR.............. 88
JOE HILL.. 20
JOHN BROWN'S BODY.........................170
John Brown's body lies a-mouldring in the grave....170
JOHN HENRY.................................... 82

KEVIN BARRY...................................194

LEAVE HER, JOHNNY.........................114
LET US ALL SPEAK OUR MINDS.............195
'Leven cent cotton and forty cent meat............104
LIFE IS A TOIL.................................136
Long-haired preachers come out every night........155
LOW BRIDGE, EVERYBODY DOWN...........115

MAN THAT WATERS THE WORKERS'
    BEER, THE.................................158
MAN'S A MAN FOR A' THAT, A..............186
MARSEILLAISE, THE..........................183
MEN OF THE SOIL........................... 94
Men of the soil! We have labored unending........ 94
Men tell us 'tis fit that wives should submit........195
MILL WAS MADE OF MARBLE, THE........... 76
Mine eyes have seen the glory....................172
MINER'S LIFE, A.............................. 65
MY SWEETHEART'S THE MULE IN
    THE MINES................................ 64
My sweetheart's the mule in the mines............ 64

NEW JERUSALEM, A..........................182
NO IRISH NEED APPLY.......................152
NO MORE AUCTION BLOCK.................173
No more auction block for me....................173
No more moaning................................164
Now some people say a man's made out of mud.... 52

O FREEDOM....................................164
Oh, the candidate's a dodger....................150

Oh, the farmer comes to town..................... 96
Oh, those West Virginia hills..................... 56
Oh, what is that I see yonder coming?............. 34
"Oh, where are you going," said Milder to Malder..175
Oh, why don't you work like other men do?........126
OLD CHISHOLM TRAIL, THE.................122
OLD MA BELL................................. 42
Old Ma Bell, she ain't what she used to be........ 42
Old man Sargent sitting at the desk.............. 74
ON THE LINE.................................. 30
One battle is won but the fight's just begun........ 78
One day as I wandered...........................136
ONE HAPPY SWEDE...........................110
One of these mornings bright and fair............. 40

PAT WORKS ON THE RAILWAY.............. 84
PEATBOG SOLDIERS, THE.....................192
PLANTING RICE...............................102
Planting rice is never fun........................102
PREACHER AND THE SLAVE, THE...........155

RED FLAG, THE...............................190
RICH MAN AND THE POOR MAN, THE.......148
ROLL THE UNION ON.......................... 44

SCABS CRAWL IN, THE........................ 46
Sh-ta-ra-dah dey...............................154
SIXTEEN TONS................................ 52
SO LONG, IT'S BEEN GOOD TO KNOW YOU...107
SOLIDARITY FOREVER........................ 12
Some people say a teacher is made out of steel......141
SONG OF THE GUARANTEED WAGE, THE.....162
SOUP SONG, THE..............................130

TAKE THIS HAMMER......................... 80
Take this hammer and carry it to the captain....... 80
TALKING UNION.............................. 22
TEACHER'S LAMENT, THE....................141
The boll weevil is a little black bug.............. 98
The boss came up to me with a five-dollar bill..... 28
The bosses are taking it on the chin.............. 31
The gloomy night before us flies.................188
The ore is waiting in the tubs....................134
The people's flag is deepest red..................190
The scabs crawl in and the scabs crawl out........ 46
The union is behind us; we shall not be moved..... 38
The union is the place for me.................... 30
The workers on the SP line to strike sent out a call. 43
The world today is mourning the death of
    Mother Jones............................... 58
There once was a union maid..................... 17
There was a rich man and he lived in Jerusalem....148
THESE THINGS SHALL BE!....................174
These things shall be! A loftier race.............174

TIMES IS MIGHTY HARD.....................154
'Tis advertised in Boston.........................112
TOO OLD TO WORK...........................143
'Twas in the town of Jacksboro....................120

UAW-CIO 90
UNION MAID 17
UNION MAN 62
UNION TRAIN 34
UNITED STEELWORKERS ARE WE........... 92

'Way back in the days of depression..............130
WE ARE BUILDING A STRONG UNION......... 72
We are building a strong union................... 72
WE ARE MARCHING ON TO VICTORY........165
We are marching on to vict'ry....................165
We ask not that the slave should lie..............167
We meet today in freedom's cause............... 36
WE SHALL NOT BE MOVED................... 38
WE WILL OVERCOME........................ 33

We will overcome................................ 33
We're brave and gallant miner boys.............. 26
WEST VIRGINIA HILLS, THE................. 56
When I makes the workers' beer.................158
When Israel was in Egypt's land..................168
When John Henry was a little baby............... 82
When the union's inspiration..................... 12
WHEN WILT THOU SAVE THE PEOPLE?......180
When wilt Thou save the people?.................180
WHICH SIDE ARE YOU ON?................... 54
WINNSBORO COTTON MILL BLUES........... 74

You work in the factory all of your life...........143
YOU'VE GOT TO GO DOWN AND JOIN
        THE UNION............................... 25
You've got to go down and join the union.......... 25
Ye sons of France awake to glory.................183

ZUM GALI GALI..............................106
Zum gali gali...................................106